Identity theft /
364.16 STE

264

Stewart, Gail B.
Charles S. Seymour Jr. Highw

W9-BXY-750

DATE DUE

NOV 18 '09			
NOV 18 '10			
DEC 03 '10			

HIGHSMITH #45115

Discard

Identity Theft

by Gail B. Stewart

LUCENT BOOKS

An imprint of Thomson Gale, a part of The Thomson Corporation

THOMSON

GALE

Detroit • New York • San Francisco • New Haven, Conn. • Waterville, Maine • London

Research for this book included interviews conducted in confidentiality, and the names or other identification of some interviewees are withheld by mutual agreement.

© 2007 Thomson Gale, a part of The Thomson Corporation.

Thomson and Star Logo are trademarks and Gale and Lucent Books are registered trademarks used herein under license.

For more information, contact
Lucent Books
27500 Drake Rd.
Farmington Hills, MI 48331-3535
Or you can visit our Internet site at http://www.gale.com

ALL RIGHTS RESERVED.
No part of this work covered by the copyright hereon may be reproduced or used in any form or by any means—graphic, electronic, or mechanical, including photocopying, recording, taping, Web distribution, or information storage retrieval systems—without the written permission of the publisher.

Every effort has been made to trace the owners of copyrighted material.

LIBRARY OF CONGRESS CATALOGING-IN-PUBLICATION DATA

Stewart, Gail B.
  Identity theft / by Gail B. Stewart.
      p. cm. — (Crime scene investigations)
  Includes bibliographical references and index.
  ISBN 978-1-59018-977-1 (hardcover)
  1. Identity theft—United States. 2. Criminal investigation—United
States. I. Title.
  HV6679.S74 2007
  363.25'963—dc22

                                                                        2007015821

ISBN-10: 1-59018-977-9
Printed in the United States of America

Contents

Foreword

The popularity of crime scene and investigative crime shows on television has come as a surprise to many who work in the field. The main surprise is the concept that crime scene analysts are the true crime solvers, when in truth, it takes dozens of people, doing many different jobs, to solve a crime. Often, the crime scene analyst's contribution is a small one. One Minnesota forensic scientist says that the public "has gotten the wrong idea. Because I work in a lab similar to the ones on *CSI*, people seem to think I'm solving crimes left and right— just me and my microscope. They don't believe me when I tell them that it's the investigators that are solving crimes, not me."

Crime scene analysts do have an important role to play, however. Science has rapidly added a whole new dimension to gathering and assessing evidence. Modern crime labs can match a hair of a murder suspect to one found on a murder victim, for example, or recover a latent fingerprint from a threatening letter, or use a powerful microscope to match tool marks made during the wiring of an explosive device to a tool in a suspect's possession.

Probably the most exciting of the forensic scientist's tools is DNA analysis. DNA can be found in just one drop of blood, a dribble of saliva on a toothbrush, or even the residue from a fingerprint. Some DNA analysis techniques enable scientists to tell with certainty, for example, whether a drop of blood on a suspect's shirt is that of a murder victim.

While these exciting techniques are now an essential part of many investigations, they cannot solve crimes alone. "DNA doesn't come with a name and address on it," says the Minnesota forensic scientist. "It's great if you have someone in custody to match the sample to, but otherwise, it doesn't help. That's the investigator's job. We can have all the great DNA evidence in the world, and without a suspect, it will just sit on the shelf. We've all seen cases with very little forensic evidence get solved by the resourcefulness of a detective."

While forensic specialists get the most media attention today, the work of detectives still forms the core of most criminal investigations. Their job, in many ways, has changed little over the years. Most cases are still solved through the persistence and determination of a criminal detective whose work may be anything but glamorous. Many cases require routine, even mind-numbing tasks. After the July 2005 bombings in London, for example, police officers sat in front of video players watching thousands of hours of closed-circuit television tape from security cameras throughout the city, and as a result were able to get the first images of the bombers.

The Lucent Books Crime Scene Investigations series explores the variety of ways crimes are solved. Titles cover particular crimes such as murder, specific cases such as the killing of three civil rights workers in Mississippi, or the role specialists such as medical examiners play in solving crimes. Each title in the series demonstrates the ways a crime may be solved, from the various applications of forensic science and technology to the reasoning of investigators. Sidebars examine both the limits and possibilities of the new technologies and present crime statistics, career information, and step-by-step explanations of scientific and legal processes.

The Crime Scene Investigations series strives to be both informative and realistic about how members of law enforcement—criminal investigators, forensic scientists, and others—solve crimes, for it is essential that student researchers understand that crime solving is rarely quick or easy. Many factors—from a detective's dogged pursuit of one tenuous lead to a suspect's careless mistakes to sheer luck to complex calculations computed in the lab—are all part of crime solving today.

A Crime Without a Scene

When Brendan Peterson walked into a downtown Chicago jewelry store in December 2004, he was very excited. "I was going to buy a ring," he says. "I was going to propose to my girlfriend, Mara, on Christmas Eve, so I was running over to the store during my lunch hour. She didn't know I was proposing that soon—it was going to be a big surprise."[1]

Brendan found a ring he knew Mara would love. He decided to charge the purchase and handed the salesperson his Visa card. Brendan remembers thinking about how he was going to propose to Mara while the salesperson went into the store office to handle the credit card transaction. She came back a few minutes later, however, and said there was a problem. The charge on his Visa card had been denied.

Brendan was certain that this was a simple mistake, that the salesperson had somehow entered the credit card number incorrectly. "I called the customer service number [of the credit card company] from the store," he says. "I was told that I had several other [Visa] cards—even the one I only use for business—that were maxed out, and that they would not accept a charge from me. It wasn't a mistake."[2]

A Crime Epidemic

Brendan is a victim of identity theft. This crime occurs whenever someone signs another person's name or uses another person's bank account, credit card numbers, or other sensitive information, usually for profit. "Since there were banks, people have been practicing identity theft," says Terry, a police investigator. "They've stolen checks, pretended to be the account holder, and have gotten money that isn't theirs. It's nothing new."[3]

IDENTITY THEFT

Has someone taken over your good name?

Protect yourself with these easy steps:

Don't leave mail in your mailbox overnight or on weekends.

Deposit mail in U.S. Postal Service collection boxes.

Tear up unwanted documents that contain personal information.

Review your consumer credit report annually.

ID THEFT

**When Bad Things Happen
To Your Good Name**

*A poster designed to educate
the public about identity theft.*

For more information on identity theft, visit

www.usps.com/postalinspectors

If you are a victim, call the ID Theft hotline at **1-877-987-3728**

7

What is new, Terry explains, is the way modern identity thieves are operating in the twenty-first century. "It's not just forging your name on a check," he says:

> In fact, though it's very common, ID theft by using someone's checkbook is considered pretty old-school, as crimes go. Nowadays, it's people stealing your credit card number and running up thousands of dollars at Best Buy, or creating new identities with fake passports and driver's licenses. And it's the people who hijack your computer and get sensitive information from your hard drive—all without you knowing it.[4]

Experts say that identity theft is one of the fastest-growing crimes in the United States. More than 10 million people were victimized by an identity thief in 2004, and investigators expect that number to increase in the coming years. Faced with the explosion of new cases in the United States, investigators who once aimed to reduce the rate of identity theft are now focused on just slowing the increase.

"That's an Extra $1,500 I'll Never See"

The consequences of identity theft can be financially devastating in several ways. First, many victims find themselves forced to pay for purchases they never made. "I was an idiot," says Samantha, a Minneapolis teacher:

> I wasn't paying attention to my [credit card] statements every month. I didn't want to be reminded of all the stuff I'd charged. Kind of just closed my eyes, and wrote the check every month for the minimum payment.
>
> Anyway, for eight months, somebody was charging stuff on my card. Nothing huge—otherwise I would have spotted it. Just a couple hundred here and there. By the

time I really paid attention, [the thief] bought more than $1,500 worth of stuff. Mostly makeup and hair products. If I'd told the card company earlier, they said they might have been able to do something about it—freeze my card, or whatever. But since those purchases were mixed up within my own, they wouldn't do anything. So that's an extra $1,500 I'll never see, I guess.[5]

A Very Frustrating Process

Some victims manage to get banks or credit card companies to forgive the charges made by the thieves, but this process can be time-consuming. In fact, the average identity theft victim in 2005 spent between fifty and sixty-five hours on the telephone with banks, credit bureaus, and merchants. Even when bank charges are forgiven, however, there are often businesses that will not reimburse victims for merchandise bought with fake credit cards. Many victims must pay fees to reinstate credit cards, or for bounced checks. They sometimes need to retain lawyers during this time, too. Because of such expenses, ID theft victims lose an average of fifteen hundred dollars. This process is even more difficult for many victims who are viewed with suspicion or as somehow at fault by customer service agents and bank officials. "I don't know of many crimes where the victim has to convince people she's the wronged party," says Samantha. "I had to keep telling my story to different people, and they'd switch me to someone else, and I'd have to tell it all over again. I didn't get a lot of sympathy, that's for sure."[6] Another victim, Chris Scurlock of Maryland, agrees wholeheartedly: "Every person I talk to has been skeptical, condescending, and hostile."[7]

All insist that the process of repairing the damage of identity theft is exceedingly stressful, with no guarantee of a satisfying resolution. Even if fraudulent charges are forgiven or stolen cash is replaced by banks and credit card companies, many victims of stolen identity suffer other damaging financial consequences. For example, their credit rating, which is largely based on their prompt payment of bills and loans, often plummets.

As one victim says, "Let me tell you that it was like trying to herd cats or put toothpaste back in the tube to undo the damage done to my credit."[8]

A person with a low credit rating is considered a high-risk borrower, less likely to get loan approval and more likely to pay higher interest rates even years after the crime. Identity theft victims are thus doubly penalized. "It's a terrible crime,"

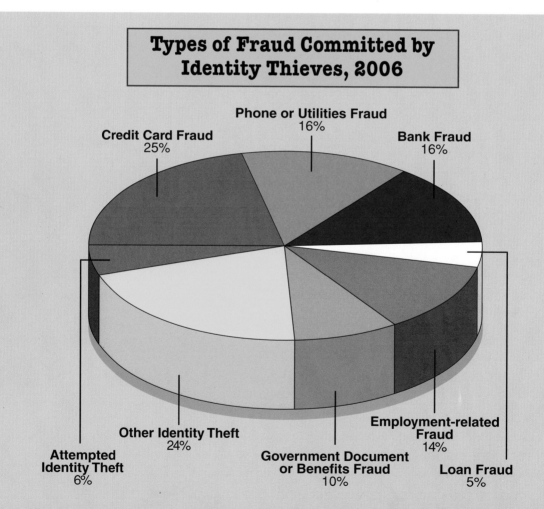

Types of Fraud Committed by Identity Thieves, 2006

- **Phone or Utilities Fraud** 16%
- **Bank Fraud** 16%
- **Credit Card Fraud** 25%
- **Other Identity Theft** 24%
- **Attempted Identity Theft** 6%
- **Government Document or Benefits Fraud** 10%
- **Employment-related Fraud** 14%
- **Loan Fraud** 5%

*Percentages are based on the total number of complaints in the Identity Theft Data Clearinghouse. Some complaints include more than one type of identity theft.

Source: Federal Trade Commission, *Identity Theft Victim Complaint Data January – December 2006*, February 2007. Available online at http://www.consumer.gov/sentinel/pubs/Top10Fraud2006.pdf.

The FBI is sometimes involved in computer crime cases such as identity theft.

dollar problem,'" he recalls. "They're not going to drop a million-dollar case to come investigate your $50,000 problem."[14]

But despite the lack of investigative resources and the staggering rise in reported crimes, many cases of identity theft do get solved. Most of those cases do not hinge on scientific breakthroughs in the crime lab. Instead, as the number of identity thefts involving computers grows, detectives must develop new investigative techniques and follow new kinds of evidence trails. Increasingly, they rely on the latest electronic-security software and diagnostic tools.

"You've got to remember that the bad guys have a lot of the same tools," says one Minneapolis investigator:

> And just when we think we're getting a little bit ahead of the game, they come up with a new way to grab sensitive information they have absolutely no business having. ID theft is a constant war against a criminal we may never see face-to-face—we will probably not catch most of them. But in many ways, it's a huge victory if we can just prevent them from ruining people's lives.[15]

CHAPTER 1

Bank Identity Theft

Check fraud is the most low-tech version of identity theft. Basically, it victimizes bank account holders, who identify themselves every time they write a check. A store or other business that accepts personal checks trusts that a customer who writes a check to pay for merchandise is actually the person whose name is on the check, the "owner" of the funds in that bank account. Anyone who uses another person's checks is guilty of identity theft. Unfortunately, check fraud is very common and very successful. Laura, a forty-four-year-old business owner from Boston, can testify to this. Laura has always prided herself on being careful with her finances, so she was appalled when she realized in November 2004 that she had become the victim of an identity thief.

"Just Signed My Name and Went Crazy"

"I am still not sure exactly how it happened," Laura admits. "Maybe at the grocery store. My purse was probably open because I was looking for my grocery list, and I turned away for a minute. That's all it takes." She says she was not even aware that her checkbook was taken, because she was paying with her bank debit card: "I don't even use my checkbook that often. It's a lot faster using the [debit] card. So whoever did it had an advantage over me. It was almost a week before I realized I didn't have my checkbook. And by that time, it was too late."[16]

Laura called her bank right away. The bank official "froze," or stopped, her bank account. Until the matter was settled, no

There are 1.4 million fraudulent checks written every day in the United States.

new checks would be processed. That protected Laura from incurring debt when a thief wrote more checks. However, bank officials found that in the five days between the theft and reporting the missing checkbook, more than $3,000 in fraudulent purchases had occurred. The thief had written checks on her account at discount and electronics stores throughout the Boston area, purchasing video games, a flat-screen television, and other expensive items. Laura recalls:

> He or she wrote seven checks altogether. Whoever it was evidently did not try to imitate my signature. Just signed my name, and went crazy spending my money. My biggest question was, how did this thief manage to go to all those stores and spend all that money without using an ID? I need to show it even at places where they know me. How is it a thief can skate through with seven stolen checks without anyone noticing?[17]

Stealing Checks

Experts say that there are 1.4 million fraudulent checks written and processed every business day in the United States. Some cases, like Laura's, involve the theft of an entire checkbook. But in many cases, says one Minneapolis police officer, a thief steals just one or two checks from a victim's checkbook. "That's smart, if you're a thief," he says:

By the Numbers

43

Percentage of U.S. fraud cases that are identity theft

It makes it harder for the victim to notice right away. Most people don't write the check and amount in their check register when they write the check. So if a check or two are gone, chances are the victim just figures he or she didn't record the amount. So instead of calling the bank and stopping payment on their account, the victim just thinks, "Okay, where did I write check number 3535? Was it at the grocery store, or for my kid's hot lunch program at school?" They just assume they forgot to write it down. And it isn't until the end of the month, when the bank statement comes that they realize what happened.[18]

He says that this type of identity thief is usually careful to keep the amount of the check low enough not to be questioned. "They usually keep a purchase to one hundred dollars or less," he says. "A thief knows he'd better write a check or two quick, before the victim finds out [checks] are missing, and tells the bank to freeze the account. It's a race."[19]

Caught in the Checkout Line

Investigators say that the success or failure of this sort of theft is often determined by the alertness of the retail employee. Many stores routinely require a second form of identification, such as a driver's license with the owner's photograph, when a customer pays by check. The chance that the check is stolen is low if the information on the check and secondary ID matches, and the photograph appears to be that of the person writing the check. Surprisingly, however, even when a thief presents his or her own driver's license along with a stolen check, many clerks don't notice that the name on the check and the name on the license do not match.

"This is really disturbing, but it happens every day," says Raymond, a manager of a large grocery store:

Clerks are overworked and busy. They've got lines of people waiting to check out, and they often just do a quick look at the picture—and how many people look like the picture on their driver's license anyway? Though they are trained to compare the address on the check to that on the license, many don't. A lot of the time the clerk is more interested in making sure the check

17

amount is right. So the customer gets through without a hitch.[20]

An alert clerk who spots a discrepancy can make all the difference. Tonya, who has worked as a cashier and clerk at a Chicago discount store, says that she scared away an identity thief trying to pass a fraudulent check.

"I remember she just had the hardest time writing the name on the check. She was looking up at the top of the check, and

A woman writes a check to pay for groceries. An alert store clerk can sometimes spot a fraudulent check right away.

then back down on what she was writing, like she was trying to copy it right or something like that." Feeling uneasy about the customer, Tonya called security. "They came to my register and apologized to the lady, and had her come in a room up front," she says. "That was just to get her to stay put, so they could get the cops to arrest her."[21]

Minneapolis police lieutenant Steve Kincaid says that this is exactly how check-writing safeguards are supposed to work:

> The store security will try to hold them until a squad can respond. Hopefully we can get the cavalry there in time to grab them. Sometimes a clerk will stall them by saying that the computers are down, and the customer should come back in half an hour to pick up the items he purchased. You'd be surprised—some of these guys are dumb enough to come back.[22]

Profiling as an Investigative Tool

Not every identity thief is caught in the act of passing a fraudulent check. Sometimes investigators are able to narrow a list of suspects based on their experience investigating other cases of identity theft. They know, for example, that in many cases of check identity theft, the thief is someone the victim knows—a coworker, perhaps, or even a family member.

Bank investigator Vicki Colliander has seen several cases in which a teen or adult child of the victim was responsible. "It may be an older child with a drug or gambling problem," she says. "In cases like these, a victim often suspects that might be the case, and may be unwilling for us to pursue the investigation."[23]

In other cases, the circumstances of the victim may provide clues to a thief's identity. For example, disabled or elderly people often rely on others for help. "They might depend on a home health worker to come in, or a neighbor to get groceries or pick up medication from the drug store," says Joleen, a St. Paul woman who works with homebound adults. "And instead of doing their work honestly, they take advantage."[24]

Washing Checks

Simply signing a victim's name to a check is only one type of check fraud. In fact, there are two others that are more complicated and more profitable for thieves.

Washing checks is a second very common form of check identity theft. A washed check is one that has been honestly filled out and signed by its owner, then stolen and chemically altered by the thief to look as if it is payable to the thief. Many areas of the United States have seen a 20 percent jump in the number of washed checks between 2000 and 2004. Experts say that 815 million dollars worth of washed checks are passed each year in the United States.

One reason for the jump in washed checks is the ease with which thieves can get their hands on these checks. The most common method is to steal personal mail that is likely to contain a payment by check, such as mail addressed to department stores, utility companies, or credit card companies. The stolen checks are taken to a makeshift workshop, where thieves use a range of common chemicals to erase the ink on the checks. Because such solvents are sold at many drug or discount stores, their purchase would not raise any red flags with store personnel.

Typically, the name on the check's "Pay to the order of" line is changed—either to the thief's real name or to a name for which he or she has a fake identification. In many cases, the dollar amount is increased, too. Thieves are careful to leave the signature intact and any changes they make to the check are written in the same handwriting and ink color as the signature. Although using a single ink color everywhere on a check is not a requirement for a legitimate check, multiple colors of ink may raise

By the Numbers

$50,000

Amount of identity theft done in the name of golf champion Tiger Woods in 2003

suspicion in an alert employee where the stolen check is eventually deposited or cashed.

Inventing Checking Accounts

The third and most technologically savvy form of check identity theft is accomplished not by chemical alteration but with a computer scanner and a printer. By printing their own checks, with real account numbers, thieves can create business or personal checks that often look completely legitimate to most people.

Bank fraud investigator Vicki Colliander says this kind of identity theft begins with software programs sold in most office-supply stores that enable businesses to print their own checks. "There's no law that says people have to buy checks from the bank, or from those companies that advertise in the coupon section of the newspaper," Colliander notes. "You can buy check paper stock that looks exactly like the paper bank checks are

A woman paying bills. Some identity thieves steal checks from outgoing bill payments, erase the ink, and then alter the check.

21

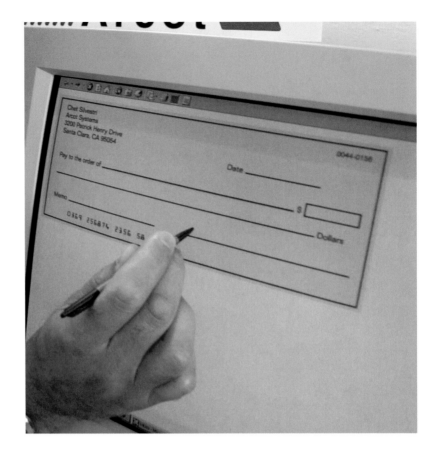

Computers allow criminals to create, alter, and print fake checks with real account numbers that often look completely legitimate.

printed on, too. The technology is out there—it's just that crooks have found a way to use it for illegal purposes."[25]

These identity thieves, like those who wash checks, rely on real account numbers. Police sergeant Sarah Nasset says that these numbers are gleaned in a variety of ways. "Sometimes it's stolen mail, like other types of ID theft," she explains. "They don't use the check, just the information on it, when they make their own. They also get numbers from hanging around the bank, keeping an eye on people making transactions there."[26]

Many identity thieves use a tactic called "shoulder-surfing," or casually standing behind a customer, close enough to read an account number or a deposit amount. Another method is simply retrieving a discarded receipt from the bank after a deposit or withdrawal is made.

Fewer Risks

By printing their own checks, criminals can easily avoid many of the risks encountered by check washers or those who simply forge another's signature on a check. For one thing, they make sure they have a fake identification, such as a fake driver's license, for whatever name they use on the check. In fact, some identity thieves have been known to possess more than a thousand different IDs, to avoid using the same name more than a few times.

For the same reason, crooks do not use the same account number for more than a check or two. They are smart enough to realize that with a few strokes on their computer keyboard, they can simply create a new check or two, with a new account number and name. In addition, they avoid suspicion by writing checks for only moderate amounts. It is rare for a cashier or teller to see if a name and account number match—usually they make sure only that the name matches the driver's license or other identification. Only when the check is processed—after it is cashed—would a discrepancy be found, and by that time, the ID thief is on to another account number.

By the Numbers

$56.6 BILLION

Cost to U.S. businesses and consumers for ID theft in 2005

In 2000 one group of identity thieves using these methods in Minneapolis had already netted more than 1.5 million dollars with their fraudulent checks—and though police knew how the group operated, they had still not made any arrests. One officer predicted that before the ring was arrested, they would have doubled their illegal earnings. "On any given afternoon, they print out a couple dozen checks and cash in $15,000 to $20,000," said Lieutenant Dana Smyser in April 2000. "Unfortunately, they're still operating and making more money as we speak."[27]

How They Get Caught

Although check ID theft is a growing crime, investigators insist that they do catch many of the bad guys. "These guys aren't superheroes," says one Minneapolis police officer. "Many of them trip up, and they are arrested. One of the most common ways they're caught is at the point where they're cashing the check. We'll get a bank teller or a cashier at a store who spots a forgery or a washed check, and that helps us out a lot."[28]

Bank tellers and cashiers are usually trained to examine a check carefully before accepting it as payment. Many times it is in the details of a check that the identity thief slips up. For example, in creating a check, the thief may not be careful about the spellings of words in the address. "Misspellings are big," agrees Nasset. "We get a lot of counterfeit checks with misspelled states, streets—even cities."[29]

Wrong Numbers

Identity thieves also give themselves away by making careless mistakes in the number sequences on the checks they forge. At the bottom of every check, for example, is a string of numbers that mean something. The checking account number is part of the sequence. The number of the Federal Reserve District where the bank is located—the United States is divided into twelve official banking districts—is another part.

If the bank whose name appears on the check is located in Louisiana, for example, the first numbers at the bottom of the check should be 11. If the check shows a different number, the identity thief has made a crucial error. An alert teller would be trained to look for a district number that matches the bank location; if it doesn't, this red flag is an important sign of identity theft.

Sometimes it is not the spelling or numbers that seem wrong, but the color or feel of a check. This is especially true with washed checks. No matter how careful a check washer is, there is usually a change in the texture of check paper that has been washed. Bank clerks who have handled a washed

States with the Most Identity Theft Complaints, 2006

STATES WITH THE MOST IDENTITY THEFT COMPLAINTS, 2006		
Rank	Victim State	Complaints Per 100,000 Population
1	Arizona	147.8
2	Nevada	120.0
3	California	113.5
4	Texas	110.6
5	Florida	98.3
6	Colorado	92.5
7	Georgia	86.3
8	New York	85.2
9	Washington	83.4
10	New Mexico	82.9

Source: Federal Trade Commission, *Identity Theft Victim Complaint Data January – December 2006*, February 2007. Available online at http://www.consumer.gov/sentinel/pubs/Top10Fraud2006.pdf.

check describe the feel as fuzzy—distinctly different from the smooth surface of a legitimate check.

Getting Greedy

Even the most well-organized identity thieves give in to the temptation to cut corners. "They go to the well too many times," says Terry, who has been involved in the arrests of several check rings. "They may start out with the idea that they will only cash X number of checks in an area per week, or will only make the checks out for a particular amount. But things go so well, they sometimes get kind of greedy."[30]

This is how police in Mississippi were able to arrest a large check ring in 2000. Investigator Andy Taylor says that two members of the ring were arrested with twelve counterfeit payroll checks in their possession. "They had a map of Mississippi with a route planned out and cities along the way circled," he says. "Similar checks which they had already passed were found in several of the cities circled on their route."

Taylor says that the two made a crucial mistake by going to the same store twice. "The owner was already suspicious from the first checks, so when they showed up the second time," Taylor explains, "he called police."[31]

Latent Prints

Though most crime scene scientific techniques are useless in identity theft cases, fingerprinting is one forensic tool that can

Latent fingerprints can be some of the most damaging evidence in fraudulent check cases.

occasionally be valuable. Many people do not realize that they leave their fingerprints on paper—including checks. They incorrectly assume that because a fingerprint is not visible, it does not exist. However, some of the most damaging fingerprint evidence is completely invisible to the naked eye.

In some identity theft cases in which significant amounts of money are being lost and cashiers are unable to spot the crooks in the act of passing checks, investigators look for fingerprint evidence. Many of the cases have been put on hold until there are more clues. A fingerprint on a bad check can sometimes provide just the clue investigators need.

"What is found on a check or other paper is a latent print," explains fingerprint expert David Peterson. "The thing is, the oils, the amino acids, the stuff that makes up a fingerprint, it soaks into the paper." By spraying a mist of certain chemicals on the check, says Peterson, the prints can become easily visible. It doesn't even matter if the check is damaged or wet—there is almost always a chemical that will help. For example, ninhydrin is frequently used to bring out latent prints on paper. However, when ninhydrin does not provide a clear print, technicians may try silver nitrate. "We've got lots of choices—in all, forty-five different chemicals for different situations," says Peterson. "Often you try one, if it doesn't work well, you try something else that's more sensitive."[32]

Of course, a check acquires many fingerprints during processing. Fingerprint examiners often ask bank workers, tellers, or cashiers for their prints first, so they can quickly be eliminated as suspects. And if they are lucky, they'll find one print that doesn't match any of those people.

But even the clearest fingerprint is of no use unless there is a suspect with whom to compare it. Prints from a bad check can be compared with a suspect's prints. If there is no suspect, technicians run the print through a huge national database of known fingerprints called the Integrated Automated Fingerprint Identification System, or IAFIS. The database contains the fingerprints of more than 65 million people. Most

Developing a Latent Print on a Check

1 Wearing a latex glove so as not to leave her own fingerprints, a technician identifies the item that is likely to have latent, or hidden, prints. Sometimes shining a special light on the surface of the check will reveal the presence of fingerprints.

2 She sprays a fine mist of a chemical called ninydrin onto the check surface. Ninhydrin reacts with the oils and sweat left on the paper by the fingers.

3 She uses either a microwave oven or a steam iron to apply heat to the paper. After a few minutes, any latent prints will appear a bright purplish-pink.

4 The prints are photographed to have another record of evidence. The fingerprints can be entered into a computer database, and sophisticated matching software will return results within a few minutes.

people know that fingerprints are routinely taken and scanned into the system when a person is arrested. Today fingerprints are also obtained in a growing number of noncriminal procedures, such as applying for a driver's license, passport, or government benefits. These fingerprints too are added to the database, increasing the likelihood that IAFIS will return a match for the print on a bad check.

"You Just Never Know"

Investigators emphasize that there is no one best way to solve check identity theft. "So much of the time it is a cooperative effort between different investigations," Nasset says. "It can be a fingerprint or just good old fashioned police work, talking to people, walking around to stores asking if they've seen an individual we suspect is responsible for bad checks. You just never know how it's going to come together."[33]

One thing she is certain of, however, and that is that the technology that allows criminals to create very real-looking checks and empty the bank accounts of innocent people is a very real threat. "Technology is so good, and crooks know it. Forget about being ahead of them. That isn't happening—at least not yet. Right now, police are trying hard to keep up."[34]

CHAPTER 2

Mail, Garbage, and Identity Theft

As identity theft grows in the United States, it has become clear that there is a very strong connection between this crime and the U.S. mail. In several important ways, identity thieves depend on the mail—especially as a means of acquiring new victims.

A Gold Mine

As noted, many crooks steal other people's outgoing mail, targeting mail that appears to be a bill payment containing a check. By washing the stolen check, they can replace the original payee's name with their own name or the name on a fake ID, then cash the check. However, stealing innocent people's incoming mail is even more profitable for some identity thieves.

"They can get an awful lot of information about you from the stuff you receive in the mail," says Rodger, a postal employee. "Think about the credit card offers alone—especially the ones for which you are pre-approved. And then there are the new checks your bank sends you, and the statements giving your account numbers and your balance. Add to that all the bills which list your credit card information, and it's easy to see that mail is a thief's gold mine."[35]

Investigators agree. They know that mail theft is a dangerous problem, and is considered the single most common method of stealing another person's identity. They say that many thieves go after not checks and money orders but rather information such as a Social Security number or bank account number that they can use to open new credit cards in the victim's name. "The real money's in the credit cards," says one police officer. "That's what they want. We've arrested thieves who discard the little checks in the incoming mail. They don't have time for that stuff—that's small-time. It's all about the Visas and MasterCards."[36]

Interestingly, as mail theft increased sharply at the beginning of the twenty-first century, law enforcement officials noticed a direct connection to another growing problem associated with criminal activity—addiction to methamphetamines, known commonly as meth. At first no one associated the two phenomena—after all, drug investigations and fraud investigations were handled by different divisions within police departments. But eventually law enforcement agencies throughout the United States realized the connection. "Almost without exception," says one Seattle postal inspection expert, "the people we're arresting for these types of crimes are doing meth."[37]

The connection begins with the addictive nature of meth and its physical and psychological effects on the people who

Methamphetamine is a powerful drug that can cause addicts to take desperate and illegal measures to secure money for their habit.

use it. First, experts agree that methamphetamine is highly addictive. "The research suggests that no other drug is as instantly addictive as meth," says Paul, a drug counselor. "Once—that's what my clients say. One time, and they were seriously hooked. And it's very, very difficult to get clean from meth."[38] A detective agrees: "Every single person tells me that, even when they were on other drugs, they were in control over their lives until meth. They can't walk away from it."[39]

Meth addicts need money to support their habit, and many view the crime of emptying mailboxes as a quick and relatively risk-free way to get it. Typically, they drive around during the day—especially in rural or suburban areas where unlocked, post-style mailboxes line the roadsides in front of houses—and methodically empty the contents. Some thieves work alone, but most work with a partner. With one person acting as a lookout, the other can rifle through a dozen mailboxes in under five minutes.

Mail Theft Rings

Some addicts are "boxers." Their job is only to empty mailboxes and sell their haul to identity thieves, who then sort through it for valuable account numbers and banking information. Boxers are paid between $10 to $30 for a large leaf-bag of mail. Two bags might pay enough to buy a day's supply of meth, although most addicts steal far more than that.

Other addicts band together to form their own identity theft rings. While some do the boxing, others sort through the mail. Still others process any found checks for washing and create false identification documents with personal information found in the mail. Others, now armed with the victim's credit card information, use the telephone to activate pre-approved credit cards.

Investigators say that this sort of intense activity fits the profile of meth addiction. "It's a long-lasting high," says Irene, a drug counselor and former addict herself. "Twelve, fifteen hours—sometimes more. And unlike other drugs that make

users feel spacey or disoriented, meth produces a buzz, like you have all the energy in the world. It's just right for doing little specific tasks that require lots of concentration."[40] Richard Rawson, a methamphetamine researcher at the University of California, Los Angeles, says that ability to concentrate on detailed tasks makes meth different from other equally dangerous drugs. "Crack and heroin users are so disorganized and get in these frantic binges," he says. "They're not going to sit and do anything in an organized way for very long."[41]

Tammie Carroll, a Denver mother of four who was arrested for her part in an identity theft ring, can attest to the fact that mail theft and meth were a natural match. "Anybody I knew that did meth was also doing fraud, identity theft, and stealing mail," she admits. "We helped each other out, whatever we needed to do that day. They all had their own little role. . . . Five days a week we did it. It was like a job."[42]

Some meth addicts empty mailboxes looking for items they can use to steal an identity.

The Value of Garbage

Some identity thieves would prefer to steal the mail a different way—by sifting through trash. Few people are alarmed by the sight of someone rummaging through a public trash can. Few people pay much attention to their own garbage once it is out of the house, or consider that it might contain something worth stealing. But police are well aware that much of what could be valuable to an identity thief goes from the mail box into the trash. Perhaps it is a credit card offer that doesn't interest the real recipient, perhaps a discarded insert from a bill, perhaps promotional material sent by a retailer to customers on a mailing list—all that garbage has information that could be used to steal the receiver's identity.

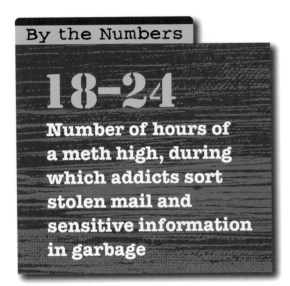

By the Numbers

18-24

Number of hours of a meth high, during which addicts sort stolen mail and sensitive information in garbage

One convicted identity thief is well aware of the value of garbage. Stephen Massey, who was arrested in 2003 for trying to pass a fraudulent check, admits to stealing garbage worth more than 1 million dollars. A businessman who had become addicted to meth, Massey first accompanied fellow addicts to a garbage dump, where they planned to scavenge for anything valuable to sell. It was the first time he had ever been to a dump, Massey recalled later, and the place was hardly appealing.

"I said, 'I'm not going to get dirty,' so I wandered over to a shed where the recycling was stored. I notice that there's a big barrel . . . that's full of discarded tax forms from an accounting firm."[43] Realizing how much more potential value there was in such information, Massey began collecting paper trash from garbage cans and dumpsters. He soon developed his own large ring of identity thieves, making hundreds of thousands of dollars each year from discarded mail and other papers that innocent people had tossed out as worthless.

Sometimes a Smaller Crime

Though mail and garbage identity thieves are prolific, they are surprisingly difficult for law enforcement to catch. In fact, many arrests are made as a result of another, less serious, crime. "We've caught them on a routine traffic stop—speeding, something like that," says Lt. Steve Kincaid. "When the officer approaches the car, he finds it full of mail—literally full of unopened mail. At that point, he realizes it's something more than a traffic violation, of course."[44]

People rarely pay attention to their garbage once it is out of the house, but identity thieves often sift through trash looking for mail they can use.

In some cases, knowing the links between meth and identity theft leads police to successful arrests. "Cooperation and communication between the cop on the street and [those investigating identity theft] is hugely important," says Sgt. Sarah Nasset. "Someone gets arrested in a drug house, and they find all these checks or credit cards, or mail, or whatever. So we get help from the cops on the streets, the ones who make arrests day after day."[45]

In one 2004 arrest in the Seattle area, narcotics detectives who raided a motel room where they knew meth was being sold discovered an entire factory for identity and mail theft. They found not only bags of stolen mail, but also counterfeit postal service keys, computers and scanners for making fake driver's licenses, and hundreds of fake checks. "People don't realize what's going on," says Ray, a retired postal worker in Shakopee, Minnesota. "This kind of thing is happening way too frequently. This has got to be stopped before everybody's identity is compromised."[46]

Caught on Tape

The likelihood of catching a mail thief in the act is slim. Even if a suspicious neighbor calls the police to report that a stranger is opening a mailbox or taking trash, it would be next to impossible for police to arrive at the scene in time to investigate, especially in remote rural areas. Even in populated suburbs and cities, unfortunately, a mail theft call is rarely assigned priority over other crimes, so it is unlikely that a squad will reach the scene in time to apprehend a suspect. The distress of being a mail theft victim several times in 2004 led one frustrated Ramona, California, man to take matters into his own hands.

Christian Davis knew that he was not the only one whose mail was being stolen. "I looked across the street and I see my neighbor's box is open as well," Davis recalls. Though he had no proof that the thieves were stealing his identity as well, Davis canceled all of his credit cards, just in case. He also filed police reports, but decided that the police could use a little help. Davis bought a special infrared camera capable of taking clear pictures even in the dark. He placed the camera in a hidden spot just a few feet from his mailbox. He also added a lot of mail to the box, to ensure that thieves would be occupied there long enough to be photographed. His plan worked. Not long after installing the camera, he was rewarded by a clear shot of an SUV with two people inside, stopping in front of his mailbox. "The lady leans out, opens the mailbox," Davis says. "I got both their faces as clear as day on tape."[47]

By the Numbers

10 MILLION

Number of identity thefts reported in the United States in 2004

Police who viewed the tape recognized the couple as suspects in other cases. With Davis's photographs as evidence, they obtained a warrant to search their house and found over one thousand pieces of stolen mail, stacked and organized. Among the letters were Social Security numbers, bank account balances, and other sensitive information. Because of the dangers involved, police do not encourage citizens to become involved in identity theft investigations. In this case, however, they were glad for Davis's help. One detective said, "His tapes cracked the case."[48]

Stakeouts

Sometimes police can actually predict where mail theft will occur. They may see, for example, that reports of mailboxes being rifled are clustered in certain neighborhoods. They may be able to determine other patterns: A thief or ring of thieves may be committing their crimes in an organized way, moving from neighborhood to neighborhood. By tracking the known criminal activity on maps, investigators can then get an idea of the direction in which thieves are moving and where they are likely to hit next.

Police can also predict that mail theft is likely to increase on certain days of the month, because bills and certain income checks are generally issued on a fixed schedule. Social security income checks to retirees, for example, are delivered each month on known dates; thieves naturally strike particularly hard on those dates.

Sometimes mail thieves are so successful in certain areas that they develop a false sense of security and do not bother to vary their routine. With this advantage, investigators have had good luck apprehending them. This was the case in Fairfax, Virginia, in 2002. After several reports of mail theft in a particular Fairfax neighborhood, postal inspectors began a surveillance operation, hoping that the thieves would hit at least one more time. At that time, a group of Nigerian immigrants were known to be stealing mail and identities, and the postal officials were reasonably sure that they were looking for Nigerians in the Fairfax case.

On July 16, 2002, their operation paid off. Members of one surveillance crew watched as a man went into a large apartment building and, using a butter knife, pried open several mailboxes and removed mail. He was arrested as he returned to his car, where the inspectors found more stolen mail, stolen credit cards, and other incriminating evidence. At least one segment of the large identity theft ring had been shut down.

No Honor Among Thieves

In many cases when a suspected mail thief is arrested, investigators know there are likely to be more people involved in

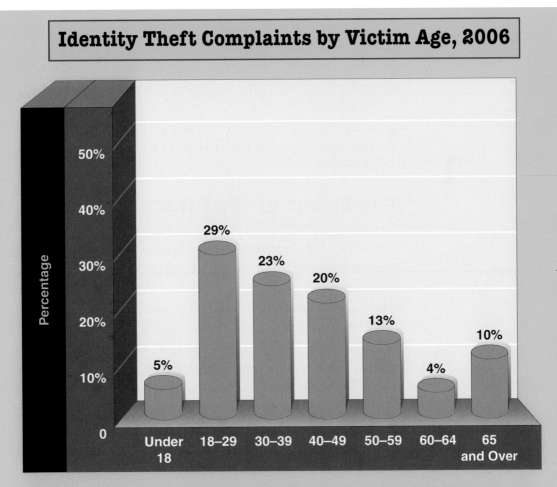

Identity Theft Complaints by Victim Age, 2006

Source: Federal Trade Commission, *Identity Theft Victim Complaint Data January – December 2006*, February 2007. Available online at http://www.consumer.gov/sentinel/pubs/Top10Fraud2006.pdf.

that particular crime. Because mail identity thieves are so often organized into rings, a suspect in custody is a valuable source of information about the ring's activities and the identity of accomplices.

Some suspects are quick to cooperate with police investigators, especially as part of a deal that reduces their own punishment. One Denver prosecutor says that addicts in particular want to avoid time in jail, where they would be cut off from their drugs. As a result, they are often willing to become informants. In his experience, he says, "It's easy to get a meth addict to flip."[49]

Other experts confirm that the old saying about thieves having a code of honor is completely wrong. No matter whether or not they are drug addicts, many identity thieves would rather receive less jail time in exchange for providing information to police. For example, Denver mail thief Tammie Carroll was finally arrested because of the testimony of a member of her ring. Carroll had been careful to adopt and discard new identities frequently, eluding detection and arrest, but a partner secretly took an identity from Carroll's trash and tried to reuse it. When she was caught, she quickly pointed the police to Carroll.

"The Power of the Interview"

Occasionally, however, identity theft suspects are initially uncooperative after their arrest. Even if police have evidence that they have committed a crime, they refuse to reveal any details about themselves or their accomplices. In cases like these, says Nasset, a police interview is an important investigative tool.

"Never underestimate the power of the interview," Nasset says with a smile. "Police can get a suspect to reveal a great deal, just by asking the right questions in the right way." She offers as an example a recent case of mail theft in the northern suburbs of St. Paul. "It was a huge case. Twenty-five victims," she says. "Officers caught a check counterfeiter, who would print checks himself after stealing banking information from someone's mail. He'd take one of his checks to the bank and write

it for cash. Anyway, he was caught after writing a bad check for $3,500."

Nasset says she was not interrogating him, nor was she being abusive or threatening in any way. "We wanted to know who he really was, where he lived, and if he was part of a ring—but he wasn't answering truthfully. I had to interview him. There are standards the criminal justice system demands," she explains, "and we are careful to follow those."[50]

A policeman shows off control panels used to monitor video of the interview room. Police can sometimes gain valuable information while interviewing a suspect.

Reading Body Language

Nasset notes that conducting a good interview depends on establishing a rhythm with the questions she asks, and especially being observant of the suspect's expressions and body

Case File: 078-05-1120

The most misused Social Security number in U.S. history is that of Hilda Whitcher. She was a secretary at E.H. Ferree, a wallet-making company, in 1939, the year that Social Security numbers were first introduced. As a way to show citizens what their card would look like in their wallets, the Ferree company made up a fake Social Security card to insert in one of its wallets' compartments. As an afterthought, company officials put Whitcher's actual Social Security number—078-05-1120—on the card, to make it look more authentic.

The wallet, which was sold in Woolworth stores throughout the United States, was a hit. But even though the card was printed all in red and had the word "SPECIMEN" stamped across it, people began using Whitcher's Social Security number as their own. By 1943 there were almost fifty-eight hundred people regularly using the number. Finally the government canceled the number and issued Whitcher a new one. It is quite possible that Hilda Whitcher was the nation's first victim of Social Security card identity theft.

language: "Cops can read body language like nobody's business." She explains that the trick is to keep the suspect off balance during the interview. "You want to get him to trip up. To contradict himself, or to slip up with some information that he wasn't going to volunteer. You ask him questions, go out of rhythm, go along a particular line of inquiry, and then throw a question at him you've already asked."[51]

She also maintains that the tone a suspect uses to answer, the way he or she sits, and whether eye contact is maintained all provide an experienced interviewer clues about whether the suspect is lying:

You see some people with a nervous tic, they're shaking, or sweating. Of course, that doesn't mean they are lying. It may just be the idea of being in a police station, or talking to me. So I explore that. I ask a really straightforward question, like "What is your name?" And maybe questions like that, easy ones, they look up into space when answering. But when I ask a hard one, like about the bad check they just passed, they start picking lint or something off their clothing. You get a feeling, that's all. You start sensing when they are being evasive, or just plain lying.[52]

Nasset says that there is nothing scientific about the interview, no concrete proof to look for: "It's just that you get a feeling what questions they're really uncomfortable with. In the case of my check writer, he was having a terrible time answering. I tripped him up finally—he contradicted himself, and he finally told me where he was living, how he was a fugitive out on bail, and that sort of thing. It was the interview that helped us that time."[53]

Federal Support for Mail Theft Investigation

One important aspect of the investigation of mail theft is that it involves the U.S. Postal Service (USPS), a semi-independent agency still backed by the federal government. Investigators like that, because of the government resources available and because postal inspectors are extremely good at tracking down mail thieves. In 2004 more than six thousand people were arrested and charged as a result of the investigative work of federal postal inspectors.

"People get very worked up about any identity theft," says USPS employee Rodger. "But mail theft is an issue that produces a lot of emotion in people. Since the beginning of this nation, Americans have felt very proprietary about their mail. It's private, and they take it very seriously. So postal inspectors

Postal inspectors have become extremely skilled at tracking down mail thieves.

get lots of cooperation when they are investigating these kinds of crimes."[54]

Prosecutors, too, are glad the USPS is involved in such identity theft cases. While many petty thieves get off with a short jail sentence—or sometimes, serve no time at all—for possession of stolen property, possession of stolen U.S. mail is not a minor offense. Theft of mail is a felony under federal law, punishable by up to twenty-five years in prison for each count. Investigators hope that the threat of lengthy prison terms will be a powerful tool in deterring would-be mail thieves and reducing this form of identity theft.

CHAPTER 3

Stealing Numbers

Stealing mail is not the only way identity thieves get valuable information from their victims. In fact, there is a dizzying array of ways that crooks are stealing—and selling—data from people's bank cards and credit cards in the United States thousands of times every day.

ATM Cards

When Jenny received her first bank debit card in the mail, she was delighted. She lives in rural Wisconsin, almost thirty miles from her bank. She admits it was very inconvenient to travel that far just to get cash; with her new debit card, she could withdraw money from her bank account at any ATM (automated teller machine). "My adult kids would laugh at me, tell me to get into the 21st century," she says. "But I resisted for a long time. I didn't know how to use an ATM machine. But I finally caved and ordered [a card] from the bank."[55]

Jenny says it didn't take her long to realize how convenient the card was. She began using it not only to withdraw cash from the grocery store's ATM machine, but also to pay for gas and other merchandise where ATM cards are accepted, instead of writing checks. But only three weeks after she got her card, Jenny couldn't find it.

"My husband said I probably left it in the machine," she recalls. "I guess a lot of people do that—they get distracted or whatever when they're retrieving their cash, and forget to take the card. He said that after a few seconds, the machine is supposed to 'eat' your card, so the next customer can't just take it—and so I should just call and see if someone could get it out for me."[56]

Jenny says she didn't worry much about the card, because she alone knew her PIN, the personal identification number each ATM cardholder chooses (and keeps secret) as a password that must be entered when the ATM card is used. She knew the card would be useless to anyone who didn't know her PIN. The next day, however, she learned from her bank that her card was not in the machine. She also was informed that her card indeed had been used over the previous two days to withdraw $400 from her account. If Jenny didn't make the withdrawals, the banker explained, someone who knew her PIN number did.

Shoulder-Surfing for PINs

Deposit and withdrawal receipts left behind at ATMs can be used to steal money out of bank accounts.

Jenny's predicament is not unusual. Identity theft experts see many cases in which people's savings or checking accounts are

drained by illegal use of ATM cards. Sometimes carelessness with PINs gives thieves their opportunity; a cardholder who writes the secret number on the card itself, or on a piece of paper in a stolen wallet or purse, is inadvertently giving a card thief the information he or she needs to use the ATM card. Cardholders who choose a PIN that can be guessed from widely known personal information, such as a birth date or the numbers in their street address, also make it easy for thieves to gain access to their ATM accounts. Jenny made neither of those mistakes with her PIN, however. Thinking back to the last time she used her card, she remembers a woman standing very close behind her at the ATM machine.

By the Numbers

$640

Average amount stolen from the victim of ATM card fraud

"It's often known as 'shoulder-surfing,'" says Steve, a St. Paul bank officer:

> It's a pretty basic, no frills type of theft. Someone stands behind you and watches as you use the touch pad on the [ATM] machine, enter your PIN. A lot of people are so engrossed in what they are doing, they don't see someone standing maybe a little too close. So they've got your PIN, and then sometime in the future, your card is stolen, and they're in business. They have a card and a PIN, and they can steal everything you've got. People naively think they are safe even when the card goes missing, since their PINS aren't known. But crooks steal those PIN numbers every day. In many cases, there's nothing hard about it.[57]

The Lebanese Loop

An increasing number of bank customers throughout the United States are becoming the victims of a con game at their ATM machine. The con is known to police as the Lebanese

Loop, because it was begun by Lebanese nationals living in London in the late 1990s. Experts say that like every successful con, the Lebanese Loop capitalizes on people's innocence and gullibility.

One Canadian woman described her experience at an ATM machine that cost her $500:

> I put my card in and a message came up on the screen saying the machine was temporarily out of order. A lady approached me, and told me that this had happened to her the other day, and what I needed to do was to key my PIN number in and then press cancel twice. I did this, and of course, no card was returned. I left the machine thinking that it had swallowed my card. But when I returned to [the bank] the following morning, my card wasn't there.[58]

Frantic because her card was missing, the woman went to the police, who told her she had been conned. They explained that crooks had most likely put a plastic loop-shaped sleeve into the slot in the machine where a card is placed. The sleeve prevented the machine from being able to read the numbers on her card, which prompted the machine to issue the message that it was not working. The helpful woman was, of course, a partner in the con. When the honest customer followed her advice to enter her PIN and push "cancel," she secretly noted the number the customer entered. After the customer left the scene, the crook or crooks pulled the card and plastic loop from the machine. Armed with the stolen ATM card and its PIN, they were able to withdraw money as they wished.

Other ATM Thefts

Some thefts of ATM/debit cards do not require the presence of the crook. Tens of thousands of cards are stolen each year by thieves in the United States, Canada, Europe, and Australia who use a device called a skimmer. The skimmer can elec-

tronically read the identifying information encoded on the magnetic stripe on the back of an ATM card when the card is swiped across the device.

In many instances, skimmers have been illegally attached to a legitimate ATM; a cardholder using the ATM is unaware that a skimmer is recording the data on the card during the transaction. In other cases the skimmers have been disguised as ATMs. The fake ATM is placed less than a block from a legitimate machine, which is falsely marked with an "Out of Order" sign that directs customers to the skimmer machine.

At the end of the day, the crook can retrieve the skimmer and the information stored inside it. "[Crooks] can use the magnetic stripe information and make up their own debit cards," says Lori, whose debit card was skimmed in 2001. "They can get a machine that reads the skimmer data and [they use it to] manufacture a brand new card. Except it's my account numbers on their card, and my money they take. It's really astonishing what they can do, and nobody stops them."[59]

An open keypad with large numbers can allow criminals to see and illegally use Personal Identification Numbers (PINs) needed to access bank accounts.

Video Cameras and Bad Spelling

Investigators are able to solve some ATM crimes, but often not before a crook steals thousands of dollars from unwary bank customers. In one case of a fake ATM set up in Maryville, Tennessee, bank customers benefited from the combination of an alert ATM user and a thief's inability to spell. The bank's ATM had a sign on it informing customers that there had been fraud attempts at that location recently. As a safety precaution, the sign read, customers were required to use a nearby card reader first, before using the ATM. The sign politely included the bank's apology for the inconvenience.

Bank surveillance video cameras can help prevent theft and other crimes at ATMs.

But Roxanne Coffey, who stopped with her husband to use the ATM, was not convinced the card reader was legitimate. What bothered her most was that the bank's sign misspelled the word *apologize* as *appologize*. Surely, she thought, a bank would not be so unprofessional. She told her husband her suspicions, and he used his cell phone to call the customer service number at the bank.

Bank officials told the couple that they had made no such sign, and warned them that the card reader was in all likelihood a skimmer. Though no suspect was identified in the case, Coffey's alertness prevented more customers from being victimized. Experts say that sometimes preventing theft is as good as solving a case. Investigators are aware that there is too much fraud to solve every case. However, when they are able to minimize damage before people are hurt, they look at it as a success.

That was not the case with one Lebanese Loop crook from Florida. The thirty-six-year-old landscape gardener was able to steal more than ninety-seven thousand dollars from victims in Florida, South Carolina, Georgia, and Washington, D.C., before he was finally caught. Video cameras, which some banks install near their ATMs, captured his image as he pretended to help an ATM customer whose card was stuck in the machine. Eventually a law enforcement officer recognized the man, and he was arrested.

"It's very common to see these sorts of ID thieves hit machines in more than one city or town," says Rob, a bank investigator. "It usually pays off when we talk to other banks, or other police departments. They often have seen the same sorts of cases, and may even have a suspect on film that they don't recognize—and that could match someone we're looking for."[60]

By the Numbers

$60 MILLION

Cost of ATM fraud to banks in 2005

Many identity thieves make their own credit cards or clone already existing credit cards.

Cloning Credit Cards

Skimmers are not only used in fake ATMs and card readers. Crooks use small versions thousands of times a day in the United States to steal credit card information from unsuspecting victims. And as with skimmed ATM cards, the stolen information is later transferred to other cards in a method known as "cloning."

The process of cloning is not terribly complex. It requires a machine called an encoder, which can be purchased over the Internet for a hundred dollars. Using an encoder, a crook can easily transfer the information on a credit card to any other card's magnetic stripe. Many crooks make their own cards, which are virtually indistinguishable from real credit cards. As one bank investigator notes, "It's really scary what you can do with a computer and stuff you can order from the Internet."[61] Once a crook has a look-alike card, he or she can simply use the encoder to rewrite a card's magnetic stripe to exactly match the original.

"It's really amazing—in a bad way," says one victim. "Somehow there's this mystery about that magnetic stripe, you just take for granted that it's personal, it's private, and, most of all, unique. The fact that someone could just steal that information that even I couldn't see—it's just mind-boggling."[62]

Skimming

Credit card skimming happens quickly and usually so secretly that a victim has no idea that it has been done. Security experts say that it occurs frequently in restaurants, bars, and even

Restaurants are an example where a credit card is out of an owner's possession and a person could skim, or clone, it.

even taxis, and is frighteningly easy with the tiny skimmers available today.

A common scenario goes like this: A dishonest waiter comes to a customer's table at the end of the meal and the customer hands him a credit card to pay the tab. In a moment or two the waiter returns with the card and the charge slip for the customer's signature. In that short time, however, the waiter has swiped the card twice—once on the restaurant's machine at the cash register, and a second time on a skimmer in his own pocket. Police know that many waiters and waitresses carry tiny skimmers—smaller than a person's thumb—in the pockets of their aprons.

By the Numbers

$150

Cost of a skimmer, frequently used by identity thieves, purchased online

Other experts agree, saying that skimming can occur anytime a card and its owner are separated. "You could be compromised anywhere," insists one California criminal prosecutor. "Anywhere you give your credit card and you lose sight of it, it's possible to be skimmed."[63]

Too Many Charges

It is not surprising that because of the secretive and quick nature of credit card skimming, few are caught in the act. But skimmers and credit card cloners do occasionally get caught, say investigators, often because of their use of the stolen card data.

For example, crooks unwittingly help investigators when they become greedy. One way they do this is by overusing a credit card. Identity thieves know that a credit card is not a permanent source of money. Customers who notice an irregularity on their statement—a large purchase, especially—will alert the bank or credit card company to a fraudulent transaction, and the account will be closed. A thief trying to make a purchase on a closed account will draw attention. Even though police may not get to the store quickly enough, investigators can get a video image or description from store personnel.

Identity thieves can also be apprehended when returning illegally purchased merchandise for cash refunds. One cab driver who skimmed customers' credit cards and used a card writer to clone new cards was caught this way. He began by using the stolen cards to pay for gas and other fairly small purchases. Eventually, however, he wanted more. It was when he started charging expensive computer equipment at Office Max and then returning it for cash that he made mistakes.

Store policy required him to present an ID with a return, and the thirty-two-year-old cab driver mistakenly presented a fake driver's license with a different name than his cloned credit card. When a store manager called security, the man fled. A week later, he tried again at a different Office Max; this time he was caught. He was unaware that the previous store's manager figured he might hit another store and had circulated his description and other information about his attempted fraud to nearby branches of the company. "I went to a different store," the crook said later, "but they were waiting for me."[64]

Help from Software

Some cases of credit card theft are first identified by the credit card companies themselves. Though these companies have no way of knowing whether a person's card has been cloned or skimmed, they do have ways of analyzing transactions that highlight suspicious purchases. The most common method is the fraud detection software that combs through millions of transactions daily, looking for unusual usage that might indicate identity theft.

Experts say that "unusual" is different for each customer. A purchase of a weekend spa treatment might appear on one woman's credit card a few times each year, while another woman would never attend a spa. A charge of heart medicine at Walgreen's might be normal for one customer, but highly unusual for another. So as credit card customers all over the world

A New York district attorney discusses a busted multi-million dollar counterfeit and stolen credit card ring. Fraud detection software often identifies suspicious credit card activity.

use their cards, software is tracking each purchase against other purchases each customer has made in the past. If something is red-flagged, the customer gets a call from the company to verify the purchase.

"I got a call last week," says Elliot, a twenty-four-year-old graduate student. "I'd never charged more than $100 or so at a time. But I found some ski equipment and bought more than $350 worth of stuff. The credit card company called, asked me about the purchase. I didn't realize they did that, but it's a good idea. I'd want to know if someone had stolen my card number and was shopping."[65]

Tracking Digital Footprints

One key investigative method used to track a credit card identity thief when purchases are found to be fraudulent is to follow the money trail. "It's basically numbers," says St. Paul investigator Sarah Nasset. "And anytime you buy something at a store, a gas station, whatever, there are lots of numbers generated. It's a footprint we can follow. If a fraudulent purchase was made, say, at Wal-Mart on September 2, the credit card company and the store have a record of that purchase, the time that it was made, and so on." Nasset says that in such cases, video is frequently a helpful tool in spotting the identity thief:

> Let's say the card was used, say, to fill up a car at a gas station; we can often look at the video for the time of purchase and get information there. Even though the card doesn't belong to the thief, the car likely does. So maybe we can get a license number from the video, or at least a description of the vehicle. And maybe the clerk on duty that day will remember something about the guy, or the thief on the tape will look familiar to us from other crimes. It really does happen, more times than you might think.[66]

Trying to Outwit Theft-Detection Software

The software used by credit card companies and banks to detect suspicious usage was developed on the basis of profiles of criminals' known purchases, ranking the probability of buying or not buying specific items. For example, identity thieves are more likely to use a stolen credit card to purchase hard liquor than to buy wine. Some identity thieves began trying to outwit the profiling software by adding an item to their shopping list that did not fit the criminal profile and would not raise suspicion—a CD of classical music.

Software experts noticed the trend in identity theft buying and adjusted the profile. Since 2005 credit-card purchases that combine expensive electronic equipment and a classical CD are now red-flagged.

Caught in the Act

As with other types of identity theft, many credit card thieves are caught committing other offenses. "It could be a drug stop, or the guy runs a traffic light," says Terry, a Minneapolis police officer. "You search the guy, or look in the car, and you find skimmers and card writers, and maybe a bunch of cards and receipts in other names that he has no business with. So the officer making the stop has a good day, taking [an identity thief] off the streets. Sometimes, it's just dumb luck."[67]

Hotel key cards like this one can be modified to serve as credit cards.

Police in Las Vegas had incredible luck in 2005, when they learned a new trick used by identity thieves. It was one investigators had never seen before, but one that they have been on the lookout for ever since. Police had been puzzled for months, wondering why so many of the drug addicts and other street criminals they arrested were carrying multiple hotel room key cards. At first, they assumed the cards were stolen and the criminals intended to burglarize those rooms.

Says Deputy Chief Dennis Cobb, "It was getting fairly regular that in post-arrest inventory [when the contents of arrestees' purses and pockets are removed and cataloged] we would find eight to ten key cards—all from different hotels."[68]

Room key cards have a magnetic stripe, on which the guest's name and room number are encoded. But when one Las Vegas police officer swiped one of the cards, he saw that it held credit card information. The key card had been rewritten by identity thieves to serve as a credit card, using the account number of an identity theft victim. Says Cobb, "The people who had these cards on them were using them in transactions with local businesses."[69]

Realizing that some crooks use rewritten hotel key cards to avoid being caught with someone else's credit card has proved helpful not only in Las Vegas, but in other cities in the United States. Though the fraudulent cards can only be used at gas stations and other facilities where people swipe their own cards without showing them to an employee, they can still rack up large losses for identity theft victims. "It's pretty astonishing," says one security expert. "Really, the whole face of financial crime has changed. And it seems that the identity thieves are adapting very rapidly. We've got a lot of work to do."[70]

CHAPTER 4

A Brand-New Name

Not all identity theft aims to steal someone else's money. Another kind of identity theft, in which someone steals another person's identity to avoid arrest or imprisonment, to impersonate a legal resident or citizen to get a job, or to mask one's criminal activity, is potentially even more dangerous. In the most sinister identity theft cases, a criminal may adopt a false identity as part of a plot to commit violent acts of terrorism. In none of these cases do fraudulent credit cards or checks play a crucial role. Instead, identity documents themselves are valuable: A driver's license, a passport, a birth certificate, or a Social Security card can provide an identity that enables someone, with criminal intent or not, to legally enter the United States and get a job.

Easy to Do

Security investigators are troubled by the fact that, in fact, the most critical documents allowing someone to gain entry into in the United States or any other country are the easiest for identity thieves to forge. "Twenty years ago—even less—you had to pay a real pro, an artist to copy an official document like a birth certificate or passport," says Norah, a security expert from Minneapolis. "It involved real skill to be able to make a facsimile like that. Not anymore."[71]

What has changed is the technology. Computers, scanners, and laser jet printers have made such forgery easy for thieves. The Internet, too, has played a key role in the success of document forgers. Anyone can browse government Web sites to study the formats for official documents and re-create them. Says deputy district attorney Rafael Acosta, "Now any yahoo with a printer and a computer can manufacture various forms of ID."[72]

Breeder Documents

The most useful documents for an identity thief are birth certificates and Social Security cards. These are known as "breeder documents," because they can be used in turn to acquire other important documents, such as passports and driver's licenses. For example, anyone can take a state driver's license test just by presenting a valid birth certificate.

Unfortunately, birth certificates are perhaps the easiest to counterfeit. There is no standard form for birth certificates in the United States, which makes it difficult for officials to determine the authenticity of any particular form. In fact, as of 2004 there were roughly six thousand legitimate forms, issued by a vast range of authorities from hospitals and home birth agencies to city or county registries to state departments of vital records. Few if any of these forms are exactly alike.

Sample American Social Security card.

With a U.S. birth certificate, a person can apply for a Social Security card, the second important breeder document. A Social Security card identifies individuals by a unique eleven-digit number under which a lifetime of tax records, government benefits, educational status, and other official records are filed. A Social Security number is required to legally be employed in the United States. Social Security cards thus are one of the most commonly forged documents, in demand by millions of undocumented, or illegal, immigrants seeking jobs in the United States. "It's the key that opens every door," insists one construction worker from El Salvador. "You need the Social for everything—to work, to open a bank account. They always ask you for your Social."[73]

The Market for Fraudulent Documents

It is estimated that at least 2 million Social Security numbers have been stolen and used by undocumented immigrants in getting a job in the United States. Some have been stolen from sources ranging from personnel files to online lists. One California assisted-living housekeeper stole more than 150 Social Security numbers from the personal files of elderly residents, and sold them to counterfeiters who make documents for undocumented immigrants.

There are thousands of counterfeiters who supply documents for a price. Their operations are concentrated in border states, such as California and Arizona, and in coastal states such as Virginia and North Carolina. Experts say that a new immigrant usually has to wait less than two hours for documents. One Phoenix man who admits he helps undocumented immigrants find people to sell them documents says that it's a very easy process:

A coyote [human smuggler] will call and say . . . "Can you help get this person some papers?" It's easy. I'll have a number for a guy and call him. We'll meet at the major intersection out here, say, in half an hour. I give him $50 or $100, whatever he's asking, a photo of the person, and a name. About 45 minutes later, he'll call me to come meet him on the same corner with the papers—a Social Security card and a green card [temporary work permit].[74]

Identity theft investigators emphasize that their job is far more difficult because many employers do not care whether the workers they hire are legal residents with authentic documents. "In lots of ways, it's in [the employers'] best interest to have illegal workers," says one California social worker. "They don't pay them nearly as much as they pay U.S workers, so they spend less money on salaries. Many of the companies have sort of a 'let's pretend' attitude about the whole thing. But they know that many of their workers haven't got legitimate documents."[75]

By the Numbers

$160

Average cost of a fake driver's license at Internet sites

"A Crime Without a Victim"

Many people do not see the problem with using another's Social Security number. After all, they argue, no one is using the number to steal money or hurt the original holder of the number in any way. "It's a crime without a victim," says Arnoldo, an immigration advocate from Honduras. "I borrow your number, I get a job and work to support my family. I don't hurt you in any way. It's just a number."[76]

But government and law enforcement officials, as well as many ordinary citizens, do not agree. Although it is true that many Americans don't even realize that their Social Security number is being used by another, eventually the deception could cause enormous problems. One blind California man, for example, was told the government would no longer issue dis-

Identity Theft Passport

John Doe
123 Elm Street
Jackson, MS 39202

Issue Date: 07/01/2004
Exp. Date: 06/30/2007
IDTP: 000001

has presented to the Mississippi Attorney General's Office documentation of a police report filed on 05-30-2004 in Yalobusha County, Mississippi, alleging that he/she is a victim of identity theft.

Jim Hood, Attorney General

Identity thieves don't consider the serious consequences felt by their victims. This demo identity card is often issued to victims to help them prove their identity.

ability checks to him since he had apparently started working at a construction company. Although the man was obviously not working construction, it was clear that someone reporting income under his Social Security number was.

Iraq war veteran Alfredo Toscano Jr. was unaware that his Social Security number had been stolen until he was stopped for speeding on the way to his niece's birthday party. The officer who stopped the Texas resident promptly arrested him, saying that Toscano's driver's license had been suspended for drunken driving. Toscano was incredulous. "I'd never gotten a DUI [driving under the influence] in my life,"[77] he says.

Even though he protested that it was a mistake, Toscano was jailed for nine hours until a judge examined the case more closely. It turned out that someone had used Toscano's Social Security number as a breeder document—first to get a job at a nearby meatpacking plant, and then to get a Texas driver's license. It was the thief whose license was suspended; however, it was Toscano's driver's license information that had come up on the police computer.

The Terrorist Connection

Identity theft has the potential to victimize people on a much larger scale. After the terrorist attacks of September 11, 2001, sponsored by the international terrorist organization al Qaeda, U.S. government investigators learned that at some time during their stay in the United States, all of the nineteen terrorists who hijacked planes and crashed them into the World Trade Center, the Pentagon, and a Pennsylvania field had used forged or stolen documents. In part because of passports, driver's licenses, or visas obtained from fraudulent breeder documents, they were able to enter and remain in the country while planning the September 11 attacks.

One man who was arrested soon after those attacks knows a great deal about the use of document identity theft and terrorism. Youssef Hmimssa's name was found in an apartment rented by al Qaeda members in Detroit. In that apartment, investigators found plans for further attacks, with targets ranging from Disneyland to the offices of the *New York Times*. And

A pile of fake driver's licenses. All of the terrorists involved in the September 11, 2001, terrorist attacks on the United States had used fake or stolen documents like these.

Stolen breeder documents and other identification papers can be altered by a meticulous hand to pass as authentic identification for terrorists.

while Hmimssa denies being a terrorist himself, he acknowledges that he created false documents for al Qaeda.

In his interviews with government agents, he provided information about the ease with which terrorists around the world obtain fraudulent passports, visas, and driver's licenses used to move freely to and from the United States. Hmimssa said he paid special interest to details, to minimize any danger that the fraudulent papers would be spotted. For example, he created his own ink for use in birth certificates, so that it would stand up to the ultraviolet light that some of the most careful inspectors would use to verify documents. One U.S. document expert noted that Hmimssa's work was frighteningly accurate. "In many cases," he said, "the counterfeit passport or counterfeit document looks a lot better than the genuine."[78]

Confidential Informants

By the sheer numbers of illegal documents circulating currently in the United States, it is obvious that law enforcement agencies are overwhelmed. Even so, police and other agents have found ways by which to identify and apprehend people who steal breeder documents and other identification papers.

As in many other criminal investigations, police rely on the services of confidential informants, often called CIs. A CI is a person with insider knowledge of criminal activity, sometimes a member of a criminal community but more often a nondescript guy on the street, who secretly helps police by telling them what he sees, hears, or knows about a case or a suspect. Confidentiality is essential: Once exposed, a CI's access to inside information ends and the CI risks retribution from suspects or their associates.

Cultivating CIs is a basic part of identity theft investigations. For instance, St. Paul police recently had a description of a man who had been stealing driver's licenses and using their information to create fake licenses with different photographs. Police knew the area in which the man was operating, and began talking to people likely to have contact with the suspect.

"Basically, we were talking to people on the street, in bars and places where this guy was believed to hang out," explains Sarah Nasset of the fraud and forgery unit. "It was nothing really high-tech—as I said, it's just the tried-and-true police work, walking around, taking the time to talk to CIs."[79]

Of course, not all informants offer their services for the good of the community. Some know that they can make a little money by helping an investigator with a case. "The department gives us a certain number of $20 bills for this purpose," says Nasset. "The serial numbers are written down—it's very organized. So if we get some help from a guy on the street, we can give him a little money. Maybe it's the cash, or we can buy him a hot meal at McDonald's, or a warm pair of gloves or something. It's not a lot, but it's something."[80]

Wearing a Wire

Some tips have far-reaching results. In February 2005 a caller to federal Immigration and Customs Enforcement (ICE) offices said he had witnessed workers at an upstate New York plant ripping up tax forms. The plant's supervisors had been warned several times by government officials that as many as 53 percent of their employees were using Social Security numbers that did not match up with government records. Those employees were suspected illegal immigrants and their documentation was likely stolen.

The confidential tip was an indication that the suspicions of ICE agents were probably true, that the workers were illegal immigrants using fraudulent Social Security numbers. As a result of this information, ICE used a CI at the plant to gather more proof. The informant agreed to wear a wire, a tiny microphone with which he could record conversations inside the plant.

Confidential informants often wear a wire transmitter to record conversations as incriminating evidence.

The informant was able to gather incriminating evidence. He even recorded a plant manager confiding what ICE suspected—that undocumented immigrant workers had stolen Social Security numbers and were ripping up tax forms since they had no intention of using the forms. As a result of the informant's efforts, ICE agents were able to arrest more than a thousand workers at several of the company's plants around the country, an outcome that surprised even the agents. Said one, "I never thought it would get this big."[81]

Red-Teaming

Some identity theft cases have even more astonishing results, as discovered by agents of the General Accountability Office (GAO), an investigative arm of the U.S. Congress charged with tracking the use of public funds. In a type of special undercover investigation known as red-teaming, groups of investigators set out in 2002 to find out how difficult it was to get a legitimate driver's license with fraudulent breeder documents.

The GAO teams visited Department of Motor Vehicles (DMV) offices in eight states and, pretending to be identity thieves, applied for driver's licenses using fake documents. Most were obvious fakes, such as birth certificates without official seals, or printed on regular paper instead of the special stock used by the government. Some of the team members handed DMV employees birth certificates listing a date of birth different from that on the license application. A few of the birth certificates had glaring alterations such as blotting out an original name with correction fluid and inserting a new name in its place.

In all eight states, at least one agency accepted the fake breeder documents and issued the driver's licenses. What investigators found most alarming was that even when a DMV employee could tell a document was fake and rejected the application, the employee usually just handed the fraudulent papers back to the undercover investigator, instead of calling over a supervisor to report it.

When the team presented its findings at a congressional hearing, one participant said, "The shocking thing is that most states picked up they were forged documents, but never did anything about it. That means there is no risk to the person trying to obtain the false driver's license."[82] The ease with which an identity thief could procure a driver's license is particularly frightening because a driver's license is the form of identification most often presented by passengers boarding U.S. commercial airplanes, whose destructive potential was tragically demonstrated on September 11.

Closer Look

Sometimes such identity theft cases can be aided by more scientific investigative techniques. Although a forensic laboratory is not used very often in cases of identity theft, it can occasionally provide important information to investigators. For example, ICE maintains a highly sophisticated forensic document laboratory, in which seized forgeries and suspicious documents are analyzed. While a suspicious driver's license would normally not be examined by a forensic technician, a suspicious passport might be because it allows a person to gain entrance into the country. Since the terrorist attacks of September 11, ICE and the Department of Homeland Security have been extremely vigilant in looking for signs of passport fraud.

The laboratory contains databases of inks, papers, stamps, adhesives, and other materials used to make or process legitimate passports and other documents in the United States and other nations of the world. For instance, when someone presents a customs official with a passport that seems unusual or suspect in some way, forensic technicians can use scientific tests to determine whether or not the document is genuine. Using multi–million-dollar instruments that can evaluate its components down to the molecular level, forensic examiners can be very certain of a document's authenticity.

Of course, important U.S. documents such as passports have features that make them very difficult to forge or create

on a computer. One feature is microprinting, a process also used by makers of bank checks and paper money. Microprinting is the printing of text that is too small to be read by the naked eye. On a check, for instance, the line on which a person signs his or her name is really not a solid line, although it looks solid. Under a magnifying glass, it is obvious that the line is actually a long series of words. Microprinting is used on passports, too. Any official who has doubts about a passport may check areas known to be microprinted. If the person has merely scanned a legitimate passport into a computer to create a new one, the microprinting would be lost, and the copy would appear to be a blurry line, not a string of distinct words.

The newest passports contain special ink, too. Known as color-shifting inks, they make the writing appear to change color as it is tilted back and forth. Blacks change to green, and back to black. The secret is a series of layers of metallic flakes added to the ink. When the passport is tilted, light reflects off the flakes at different wavelengths. The U.S. government is the only customer of the manufacturer of this special ink. That

Forensic document laboratories can intensely scrutinize passports and other questioned documents.

means that someone trying to forge one of the newest U.S. passports could be caught by an official alert enough to notice the absence of color-shifting ink.

Doctoring a Real Document

Because of the difficulty of creating a fake U.S. passport, many identity thieves steal real passports and alter them. Stolen passports are readily available on the black market throughout Europe, the Middle East, and Asia. In addition, in recent years

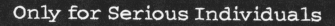

Only for Serious Individuals

The following is an excerpt from the sales pitch of an online seller of fake IDs. To avoid publicizing an enterprise that is suspect, the name of the company and its Web address are not included. The seller's claims are typical of many other online sellers of fraudulent documents.

We also offer a limited number of high-quality novelty passports each month. These are strictly on a first-come, first-served basis, due to our limited supplies at times. To get pricing for a fake passport, please contact us. We can replicate most any passport upon request and proper pricing. Our fake passports are of the highest quality and look very near identical to an official one. In addition, we can work on a one-on-one basis with you to create a completely custom passport job.

Use our fake passports in conjunction with our fake ID's for a complete 'New Identity' Package. Upon request, we can create a complete identity solution. This can include a fake novelty ID, a fake passport, and several other different forms of identification such as credit cards, checkbooks, utility bills and fake corporate documents if needed. Let us stress that creating our custom packages are only for individuals that are serious about creating complete turnkey identity packages.

authentic passports—American as well as those from other countries around the world—have been boldly peddled over the Internet.

One method identity thieves use to doctor a real passport is to use a very, very thin clear laminate over the picture and biographical data on the document. First, however, they obliterate the original photo, so that it does not show through the laminate, and create a double image. The laminate contains a new picture (of the thief). While ICE officials do not wish to provide details about the method, they say that they have been successful in stopping such fraudulent passports because the laminate layer is never placed exactly over the original page. A slightly ragged edge where the laminate hangs over the edge of the page alerts a border official, and the forensic lab can verify that it is a fake.

With new technology being developed for creating documents, national security experts hope that they can slow down the use of faked copies. They realize that the stakes are high. The danger is not so much failing to prevent an immigrant from illegally entering the United States in search of a better life, they say, but failing to prevent an enemy from crossing the borders of the United States intending to commit an act of terrorism.

Stolen passports are readily available in many places throughout Europe, the Middle East, and Asia.

CHAPTER 5

Online Identity Theft

While all forms of identity theft are increasing, investigators report that the number of cases in which computers are used is growing at the most rapid pace. Identity theft experts estimate that computers are used in nearly 45 percent of all identity crimes. According to the FBI, in fact, in just one year, from 2003 to 2004, computer identity crime increased 66.6 percent. Each year since, it has been rising at a similar rate.

"You Don't Have to Carry a Gun"

Computers are such an essential tool in business activity and personal communication today that experts say it is almost impossible to embezzle money, buy and sell stolen credit card numbers, or commit other types of business or identity fraud without targeting and using a computer. Moreover, criminals are increasingly turning to computer crime—also called cybercrime—because cybercrime is relatively safe. Thefts on a huge scale can be carried off from the thief's home, without ever confronting a victim. "There's a lot more money [in it] than burglary," says one investigator, "and it's safer for them; you don't have to carry a gun."[83]

Unfortunately for law enforcement agencies, the risk of being apprehended is minimal too. Although there are certainly talented investigators with the tools necessary to solve such crimes, police departments are overworked and usually greatly understaffed. Typically, solving one computer crime requires the use of between twenty and twenty-five computers, and most law enforcement agencies cannot divert the time and manpower away from investigations of violent crimes.

Another challenge in solving cybercrime is the lag time between when a person or business is victimized and when they realize that a crime has taken place. Even the largest corporations tend to be unaware of being victimized. That, says one computer expert, is the nature of the crime. "It used to be that if I were to break into your safe and steal the $1 billion that your company had there," he says, "you would notice it was missing. Today, if I intelligently come into your virtual [computer] safe and steal your intellectual property, you don't know that I've taken it, nor do you know what I'm going to do with it and how it's being used until you begin to see symptoms."[84]

"That's the Nightmare Scenario"

But even with such difficulties inherent in computer identity theft, investigators realize that it is a serious crime that cannot be ignored. Tens of billions of dollars are lost to cyber-thieves

Computers are so prevalent in crimes today that police departments often assign officers full time to monitor cybercrime.

By the Numbers

$400

Hourly rate of a forensic computer technician in the private sector

each year as computer thieves steal corporate records and personal information about millions of credit card customers. They impersonate legitimate businesses to steal consumers' Social Security numbers and bank account numbers. They move in and out of Internet chat rooms as they buy and sell that stolen identity data to other thieves.

But many businesses say that there is even a more ominous effect of computer identity theft than the massive amounts of money lost each year. "Most worrisome is the long-term effect of cybercrime," says Barbara Kramer, a Chicago marketing executive. "It's the lack of confidence that people will get in online businesses. They will worry a company's Web site is not safe, that their personal information will be compromised. No one wants to feel unsafe when they shop. If those fears become increasingly common, that will hurt business in this country dramatically. That's the nightmare scenario."[85]

Targeting Oprah and Steven Spielberg

Experts insist that anyone can be a victim of computer identity theft. It seems to make no difference how wealthy, well connected, or well guarded people are—no one can guarantee their identities are protected. The case of Abraham Abdallah is a case in point. This thirty-two-year-old New York restaurant worker became fascinated with Forbes magazine's annual issue listing the four hundred wealthiest people in the United States. Using a computer at the public library, Abdallah was able to fake the identities (including Social Security numbers and other sensitive information) of about two hundred of those people, including Oprah Winfrey, director Steven Spielberg, and investment billionaire Warren Buffet.

Abdallah had few resources, but police admit he was very creative. In addition to the profile data supplied by the magazine articles, he used the Internet to begin gathering information about his victims. The rest he was able to get by pretending to work for large investment firms. For this, Abdallah relied on his mastery of one of the most valuable techniques of a good identity thief, known as "social engineering." "It's a type of manipulation," explains information technology expert Firasat Khan. "It's a way of getting people to reveal information without their being aware of it."[86]

Abdallah fast-talked secretaries and bank workers into giving him privileged information about customers. He also created genuine-looking stationery with the name of investment banks, and even had a rubber stamp made in the name of a prestigious investment firm, all touches that made his scheme very believable.

Using Internet resources Abraham Abdallah faked the identities of numerous celebrities in order to gain access to their bank accounts.

Too Much, Too Fast

By using a number of voice mail accounts in the names of his famous victims, Abdallah busied himself selling off investments and having money transferred to various accounts (also in the names of his victims), as well as opening credit cards for himself in his victims' names. As investigative reporter Bob Sullivan writes, "Using a cell phone, some voice mailboxes, and free e-mail accounts, [Abdallah] had fast-talked his way through receptionists and security questions for six months. Eventually, he had access to billions of dollars."[87]

He was caught, however, after six months, brought down by his own greed as well as the alertness of an investment banker. In March 2001 Abdallah decided to

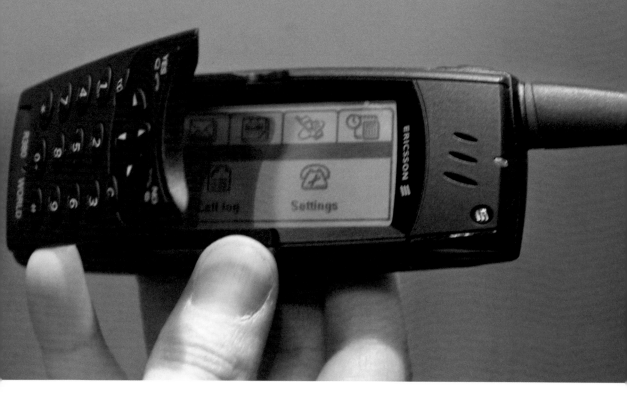

Cell phones, voice mailboxes, and e-mail allowed Abraham Abdallah to bypass security questions for months.

transfer $10 million from one victim's account at investment firm Merrill Lynch to a new account in Australia. The agent was suspicious because he had seen five other requests for transfers come from the same e-mail address on Yahoo. Once the police were alerted, they wound their way through the tangled web of e-mail addresses and voicemail accounts to find Abdallah.

Higher Tech

Though that sort of identity theft via computer was considered to be complex in 2001, say experts, technologically speaking, today it would rank fairly low on the computer crime scale. Every time Abdallah had to interact with people in the process of getting sensitive information about his victims, he was at risk of exposing himself as an identity thief.

By 2006 identity thieves had realized how much could be done in their homes or at their computer at work, armed only with software and a mouse, with little or no interaction with potential witnesses. They can hack their way into supposedly secure corporate computer systems, for example, and steal employee and customer data. They can then take that data to one of the countless, anonymous Internet chat rooms in which this information is regularly bought and sold.

While many forms of identity theft are solved because of standard police procedure—following up leads, interviewing witnesses, and so on—the majority of these high-tech computer crimes require the expertise of a new kind of forensic investigator.

"Sherlock Holmes on a Hard Drive"

For instance, though an investigation may point to a suspect, evidence or proof of guilt is usually difficult to find in a computer crime. That was certainly the case when employees began stealing important secrets from a large corporation where they worked and selling them to a foreign competitor. "In cases of computer identity theft," says one security expert, "you're

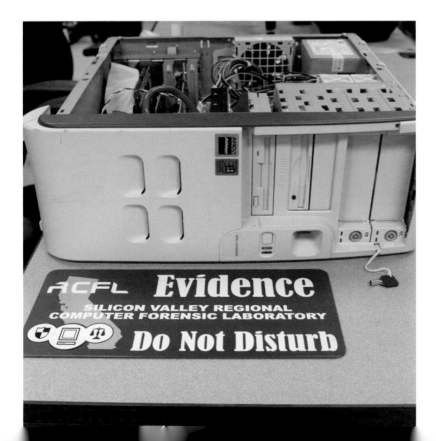

Computer forensic experts often disassemble computers to find evidence, which can take hours.

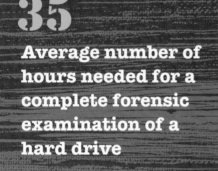

By the Numbers

35

Average number of hours needed for a complete forensic examination of a hard drive

not going to have the kind of evidence you see in most crimes. If he is guilty, the evidence will be there all right, but it won't be in the guy's pockets or in his car. It'll be on the guy's hard drive. It's up to the computer forensics [experts] to find it. If it's there, believe me, they'll find it."[88]

Computer forensics experts are not only well versed in technology, they are also investigators. One insists that his job is not merely running software on a suspect's computer that will automatically locate evidence. "It's not about being computer literate," he says. "It's about investigative skills and being able to think like a crook. There isn't a black box that finds fraud."[89] David Wilson, another computer forensics expert, could not agree more, saying, "We're kind of like Sherlock Holmes on a hard drive."[90]

In the case of corporate employee theft, the case depended on a careful search through the inner workings of the suspect's computer. In such cases, it is crucial that the suspect not be aware that his or her work computer is being examined, so investigators must work secretly, either at night or some other time when the employee is not present. In a process more like something out of a spy movie than a police investigation, forensics experts take photographs of the suspect's desk and computer, so that the workspace can be perfectly restored to its previous condition when the investigators leave.

Securing the Crime Scene

Because the forensic examination of a hard drive can take many hours, the forensics workers do not carry it out on site. Instead, they make a copy, using special software that does not add or delete anything. That is important, say experts, because the tiniest detail that is altered will affect how the evidence will later stand up in court.

"For the same reason crime lab techs are careful not to touch anything at a crime scene without gloves, [computer forensics workers] have to keep the evidence exactly as it is found," says Peter Olsen, a security expert. "It's keeping the chain of evidence clean, not letting it become contaminated by any examiner or outside influence. Otherwise, that contaminated evidence is useless in court, and a guilty person could go free."[91]

FBI computer expert Mike Morris says that some of the biggest threats to keeping computer evidence clean are well-intentioned detectives. "They think they know how to use a Mac or Windows," he says, "so they fire up the computer and click through it. It's equivalent to walking through the crime scene."[92]

Digital Footprints

Finding incriminating evidence on a computer hard drive can be a long, arduous process. What investigators search for can best be described as "digital footprints"—clues that are left by the person using the computer that point to a specific crime. The evidence can be found either in looking at the activity of the user—which can be identified by an expert—or by the data found in files, folders, and programs in the machine.

In the case of the employees suspected of selling corporate secrets to a foreign company, forensics experts found evidence that the employees had lied during an interview. They had said that they knew no one in that foreign corporation, yet their computers had parts of corporate documents that had been translated into the language of the foreign competitor. Even more damning, forensics expanded their search to an examination of one suspect's Palm Pilot, and found the competitor's name and contact information. This was all

By the Numbers

90

Percentage of U.S. corporations that experienced some computer crime between 2003–2006

the evidence needed for investigators to apprehend the employees for a computer crime.

"It's Not Really Gone"

Sometimes identity thieves put too much faith in the idea of deleting, or erasing, files. That can be a break for investigators, who know that when a file is deleted, it is still on the computer's hard drive. One expert says he really enjoys seeing the scramble to erase files when employees hear a forensic computer investigator is going to be looking at their hard drives. "When users in corporations hear [an investigator] is coming in, they try to 'Tidy Bowl' their hard drives," he says with a smile. "Computer forensics people love this."[93]

Minneapolis technology expert Firasat Khan says that such actions don't usually work because there is so much empty storage space on a hard drive. "Lots of space [on a hard drive] is

Even after files have been deleted, investigators can still retrieve those files on a computer's hard drive.

not used," he explains. "Now, when you delete the file, that's like the index card that has information on where each piece of the file is. That's what you're really throwing away, not the file. Afterwards, you ask your computer, where's the file? It tells you it's gone, doesn't exist."

But the special software used by investigators doesn't bother asking the computer where the file is, says Khan. "It just goes in and reads the clusters of data in the hard drive. You'll find entire files or chunks of files still there—all of which you deleted. But it's really there."[94]

The same goes for e-mails and Internet pages—a record of every Web page that has been viewed remains. That can be trouble for someone who is suspected of sending threatening e-mails, for example, while concealing his or her identity. A forensic investigator can use software to get deep inside the hard drive and find the threatening messages, if not in their entirety, at least enough to prove that the suspect did send them.

Scary Software

Some acts of computer identity theft are stranger than others. In one 2003 crime, a man woke up in the middle of the night, alerted by the noises his computer was making. "I thought at first it was my antivirus software running," he later recalled, "and I kind of ignored it." As the noises intensified, however, he got up and looked at the screen and was astonished by what he saw.

The mouse cursor was moving by itself, darting around the desktop, opening files and appearing to be searching for something. He realized he was watching a crime in progress—a remote hacker had hijacked his computer and was looking for personal data. "I sat there as this person opened my [confidential files], and some documents in other files, and got my

By the Numbers

$85

Black-market price of credit card information for a single American Express card

Remote hackers can break into home and office computers and hijack personal data with no witnesses to their illegal activities.

Social Security number and credit card numbers."[95] As he continued to watch, the invisible thief began opening accounts and new credit cards, all in the victim's name. Finally, he touched the mouse, and the activity stopped.

Trying to figure out how a hacker could have obtained his information, the victim remembered going to a Kinko's store not long before, and using a computer there to check his e-mail. Forensics experts were able to track the computer used by the thief by its Internet protocol (IP) address—a code used by the company that provides Internet access to that customer. The company has records of a street address for each IP address.

In this case, the police found a man in New York City, who confessed to identity theft. He had installed a software program in Kinko's terminals that recorded every keystroke entered at the computers there. Periodically he would return to the store and retrieve that information, which he would use to get into other people's computers. The software, which is often used by parents to monitor their children's computer use, was simply used for illegal purposes.

"Everything Looked Exactly Right"

The fastest growing types of computer identity theft occur on the Internet. Just as Abraham Abdallah used fake letterheads and rubber stamps to make his phony letters look realistic to investment firms, Internet thieves create genuine-looking e-mails to impersonate those of a trusted company. Because people can rarely detect that the e-mail is phony, they may be tricked into giving the thief personal information, such as a Social Security number or credit card number. Such a computer scam is known as "phishing."

By the Numbers

$2.4 BILLION

Cost to U.S. consumers of phishing scams

Lon, a retired St. Paul school bus driver, was a victim of a phishing scam in August 2006. "I got an e-mail from my bank," he says. "I thought it was my bank, I should say. The e-mail had the same design, the same way of writing the name, everything looked exactly right. Anyway, it told me my account information was being updated, and I needed to send my Social Security number and my savings account number."[96] He followed the instructions.

Lon says that he read an article in the newspaper about phishing not long afterward, and began to wonder about the e-mail he had received. "I asked at the bank the next time I went in, and they knew what I was talking about. They said the bank never, ever requests that kind of information in an e-mail. And they also said that other people had gotten the same message as me. I always thought I was pretty careful, but I guess I wasn't."[97]

"We Get on a Computer and We Go into Freefall"

It was estimated in 2004 that 1.78 million Americans had fallen for a phishing scam, just as Lon did. Some responded to what looked like a bank message, others to a pension fund, and some to a government agency. Forensic experts say that phishers are experts at cloaking their own IP addresses to make it difficult for anyone to trace them.

Though investigators have methods to trace the address, it is often a waste of time. "You'll get a computer at a public library or an Internet cafe," says one. "And more often than not, the [phisher] will be operating out of someplace in Asia or Russia. There usually aren't enough resources to pursue an investigation like that, not unless it was a matter of national security or something."[98]

St. Paul investigator Sarah Nasset says the problem could better be addressed by prevention. "I wish we had more money to educate," she says. "We could eliminate 99 percent of this stuff if people just knew what to do to be safer. I mean, we lock our houses, we lock our cars, but we get on a computer, and we go into freefall. My dog's name is Spot, my dad's name is Peter—we share information like crazy."[99]

"The Wild, Wild West"

Occasionally, investigators can track an Internet thief in the process of selling the stolen data. For that, too, thieves rely on what one security professional refers to as "the Internet's shadowy underbelly"—the countless secret chat rooms where the Internet's black market flourishes, where stolen credit information is bought and sold. Some buy numbers in bulk, while

A man and a woman in an Internet café. Phishers sometimes operate from Internet cafés in order to avoid capture.

some purchase numbers and information from a prestigious Gold Visa card for $100. Because of this far-reaching lawlessness, Senator Charles Schumer of New York has called the Internet "the wild, wild West."[100]

Some forensics investigators monitor such chat rooms, hoping to get a clue about the identity of the sellers. Several investigators have taken part in undercover operations, in which they try to impersonate a potential buyer. They say that it is difficult, partly because the chat rooms move around quite often, but more because of the nervousness of the participants.

Becoming a Forensic Computer Investigator

Job Description:

A forensic computer investigator's job is to collect and analyze computer-related evidence in a criminal investigation. Sometimes this involves a computer in custody, but other times the investigator must locate the computer by tracing e-mails or other messages. In addition, an investigator is often called on to testify in any trials that involve the forensic evidence.

Requirements:

An information technology (IT) certification is necessary, as well as a college or university degree in applied science, criminal science, or a related field. A computer investigator must have good deductive reasoning skills and an ability to communicate well with juries or other laypersons who do not have the same technological expertise.

Salary:

In a police department, forensic computer investigators make between $50,000 and $70,000. In the private sector, they can earn twice that amount.

"You've got to know the language and the secret handshakes," says one expert. "Once you're in there, everyone watches everyone to see who's a fed."[101]

However, sometimes their patience has paid off. In an undercover investigation code-named Operation Firewall, Secret Service agents and forensic computer experts watched their screens as various members of an organized identity theft network talked online. Though the members would usually take time to use screen names to cover their IP addresses, at one time, someone logged on from an unsecured computer.

This was the break investigators needed. They were able to trace the criminal through his IP address. Once he was caught, he was willing to help agents identify other members of his network. In October 2004 a total of twenty-eight identity theft criminals in eight states and several countries were

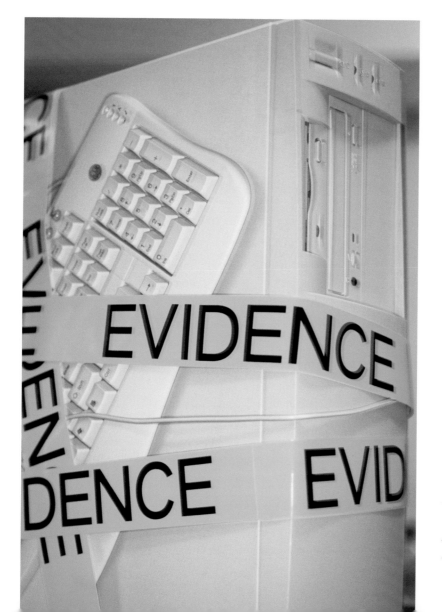

Undercover investigators can trace criminals through their IP addresses and confiscate their hard drives as evidence.

arrested, and investigators were able to get a closer look at how such networks are organized.

An Uncertain Future

Information learned in the arrest of an identity thief can help future investigations. Police and other law enforcement officials say that they are constantly revising their methods to keep up with identity thieves. Some experts are guardedly optimistic about the future. They say the creation of new forensic methods, such as software that can red-flag purchases perhaps by identity thieves, are evidence that they may someday be able to get the upper hand with these criminals.

The Unsent E-Mails

Forensic computer technicians find that most of their cases involve large amounts of money. However, there are cases in which the motive is not financial gain. In one case that took place in Minnesota in 2004, a woman filed a lawsuit against her boss, a thirty-one-year-old married man who she said had sexually harassed her. The boss denied the charge, but accused the woman employee of harassing him. To prove his point, he produced printouts of several explicit e-mails she had sent to him. He further said that she was angry with him for refusing her advances, which was why she was suing him.

Forensic investigators looked at the man's computer, but nowhere among the e-mails could they find the messages he showed them. But how could that be? The man had showed investigators the explicit e-mails. What investigators found was that the man had written the e-mails to himself, pretending to be the woman. He did not send them, of course, but printed them out, so it looked as though they were real. That evidence proved that he had lied.

Others, however, feel that it is a battle that will be impossible to win. They say there are too many organized rings of identity thieves operating out of foreign countries, where police are either disinterested or overwhelmed with other crimes. They see, too, an American judicial system that is unwilling to get tough at prosecuting identity crimes and police departments that are underfunded and unable to deal with the huge numbers of such cases.

"It's an unfortunate fact," says one Chicago bank official, "that to investigate and prosecute every case of identity theft today is not even possible—either in terms of manpower or money. That's why it's the big cases—the ones where millions of dollars are being stolen—that get the attention from investigators. And even then, there are no guarantees that law enforcement is going to be successful. Banks and police are facing too many enemies at one time." [102]

One security expert agrees, and says that the criminals seem to be adjusting faster than law enforcement. "These threats are constantly evolving and changing," he says. "I don't think we're on top of it." [103]

Notes

Introduction: A Crime Without a Scene

1. Brendan Peterson, telephone interview by the author, December 1, 2006.

2. Peterson, December 1, 2006.

3. Terry, interview by the author, Minneapolis, MN, November 16, 2006.

4. Terry, November 16, 2006.

5. Samantha, interview by the author, Minneapolis, MN, November 8, 2006.

6. Samantha, November 8, 2006.

7. Quoted in Margaret Mannix, "Stolen Identity," *U.S. News & World Report*, June 1, 1998, p. 48.

8. Quoted in David R. Brockel, "Stolen Identity," *Officer*, September 6, 2006, p. 26.

9. Sarah Nasset, interview by the author, St. Paul, MN, December 12, 2006.

10. Terry, November 16, 2006.

11. Bob, telephone interview by the author, January 7, 2007.

12. Quoted in Daniel Wolfe, "ID Theft Group Members Say Collaboration Helps," *American Banker*, February 17, 2005, p. 12.

13. Quoted in "Identity Theft: The Organized Crime Factor," Rutgers University Identity Theft Resolution Services Online, August 2003. www.identity theft911-sunj.com/articles/article. ext?sp=90.

14. Quoted in Daniel Wolfe, "Police, Banks Not in Sync on Identity Crime?" *American Banker*, September 27, 2006, p. 1.

15. Donna, interview by the author, Minneapolis, MN, January 15, 2007.

Chapter 1: Bank Identity Theft

16. Laura, interview by the author, Minneapolis, MN, November 17, 2006.

17. Laura, November 17, 2006.

18. Terry, November 16, 2006.

19. Terry, November 16, 2006.

20. Raymond, interview by the author, Bloomington, MN, November 29, 2006.

21. Tonya, interview by the author, Minneapolis, MN, January 12, 2007.

22. Steve Kincaid, interview by the author, Minneapolis, MN, March 10, 2006.

23. Vicki Colliander, interview by the author, Lake Elmo, MN, March 3, 2006.

24. Joleen, telephone interview by the author, St. Paul, MN, November 11, 2006.

25. Colliander, March 3, 2006.

26. Nasset, December 12, 2006.

27. Quoted in David Chanen, "Police Working to Stop Check Ring," *Minneapolis Star-Tribune*, April 29, 2000, p. 1A.

28. Charles, telephone interview by the author, January 6, 2007.

29. Nasset, December 12, 2006.

30. Terry, November 16, 2006.

31. Quoted in Kasey Wertheim, "Tools to Combat Check Fraud in Mississippi," Mississippi Division of the Internal Association for Identification Newsletter Online, vol. 11 no. 1, 2002. www. mdi-ai. org/Newsletters/magnolia1-1.htm.

32. David Peterson, interview by the author, St. Paul, MN, April 20, 2005.

33. Nasset, December 12, 2006.

34. Nasset, December 12, 2006.

Chapter 2: Mail, Garbage, and Identity Theft

35. Rodger, interview by the author, Minneapolis, MN, December 3, 2006.

36. Terry, November 16, 2006.

37. Quoted in Sam Skolnik, "Meth Use Linked to Jump in ID, Mail Thefts," *Seattle Post-Intelligencer*, July 23, 2001, p. 1A.

38. Paul, interview by the author, Inver Grove Heights, MN, December 3, 2006.

39. Quoted in Skolnik, "Meth Use," p. 1A.

40. Irene, telephone interview, December 13, 2006.

41. Quoted in John Leland, "Meth Users, Attuned to Detail, Add Another Habit: ID Theft," *New York Times Online*, July 11, 2006. www.nytimes.com/2006/07/11/us/11meth.html.

42. Quoted in Leland, "Meth Users, Attuned to Detail."

43. Quoted in Rob Hamadi, *Identity Theft: What It Is, How to Prevent It, What to Do if It Happens to You*. London, UK: Vision, 2004, p. 106.

44. Kincaid, March 10, 2006.

45. Nasset, December 12, 2006.

46. Ray, interview by the author, Shakopee, MN, November 1, 2006.

47. Quoted in Shannon Tangonan, "Hidden Camera at Mailbox Nabs Rural ID Thieves," *San Diego Union-Tribune*, January 14, 2005, p. 1A.

48. Quoted in Tangonan, "Hidden Camera," p. 1A.

49. Quoted in Leland, "Meth Users."

50. Nasset, December 12, 2006.

51. Nasset, December 12, 2006.

52. Nasset, December 12, 2006.

53. Nasset, December 12, 2006.

54. Rodger, December 3, 2006.

Chapter 3: Stealing Numbers

55. Jenny, interview by the author, Minneapolis, MN, December 26, 2006.

56. Jenny, December 26, 2006.

57. Steve, telephone interview by the author, January 16, 2007.

58. Quoted in "Beware of Crooks Disabling ATM Machines to Get Your Card," Truth or Fiction.com. www.truthorfiction.com/rumors/l/lebaneseloop.htm.

59. Lori, telephone interview by the author, January 6, 2007.

60. Rob, telephone interview by the author, January 16, 2007.

61. Rob, January 16, 2007.

62. Lori, January 6, 2007.

63. Quoted in CBS News Online, "Is Your Credit Card Being Skimmed?" December 6, 2002. www.cbsnews.com/stories.2002/12/06/eveningnews/main532125.html.

64. Quoted in Ann Mullen, "Cell Phony: Government's Star Witness Says He's a Scam Artist, Not a Terrorist," Metrotimes, April 16, 2003. www.metrotimes.com/editorial/story.asp?id=4801.

65. Elliot, interview by the author, Minneapolis, MN, January 22, 2007.

66. Nasset, December 12, 2006.

67. Terry, November 16, 2006.

68. Quoted in Brian Krebs, "Security Fix," Washingtonpost.com, March 6, 2006. http://blog.washingtonpost.com/securityfix/2006/03/street_level_credit_card_fraud.html.

69. Quoted in Krebs, "Security Fix."

70. Norah, telephone interview by the author, January 18, 2007.

Chapter 4: A Brand-New Name

71. Norah, January 18, 2007.

72. Quoted in Tangonan, "Hidden Camera," p. 1A.

73. Quoted in Franco Ordoaez, "Phony IDs Luring Illegal Immigrants," Hispanic Business Online, January 3, 2007. www.hispanicbusiness.com/forum/topic.asp?TOPIC_ID=9565.

74. Quoted in Faye Bowers, "An Illegal Immigration Link to Identity Theft," Christian Science Monitor, December 14, 2006, p. 1.

75. Marcia, telephone interview by the author, January 3, 2007.

76. Arnoldo, telephone interview by the author, January 4, 2007.

77. Quoted in Arnold Hamilton, "In Business of Fake Documents, Innocent People Often Hurt," Knight Ridder/Tribune News Service, November 27, 2006, p. 1.

78. Quoted in Bob Sullivan, Your Evil Twin: Behind the Identity Theft Epidemic,

Hoboken, NJ: John Wiley & Sons, 2004, p. 125.

79. Nasset, December 12, 2006.

80. Nasset, December 12, 2006.

81. Quoted in Michelle Mittelstadt and Diane Jennings, "Insider's Tip Led to Crackdown on Illegal Workers," *Knight Ridder News Service*, April 21, 2006, p. 1.

82. Quoted in Bob Hager and Bob Sullivan, "Fake Drivers Licenses Easy to Obtain," MSNBC Online, September 9, 2003. www.msnbc.msn.com/id/3078924.

Chapter 5: Online Identity Theft

83. Quoted in Jenn Stewart, "More Thieves Armed with a Mouse," *Orange County Register*, April 28, 2005, p. 4.

84. Quoted in Kathryn Jones, "Cybersleuths," *Texas Monthly*, August 2000, p. 102.

85. Barbara Kramer, telephone interview by the author, January 26, 2007.

86. Firasat Khan, interview by the author, Minneapolis, MN, December 15, 2006.

87. Sullivan, *Your Evil Twin*, p. 23.

88. Norah, January 18, 2007.

89. Quoted in Jones, "Cybersleuths," p. 102.

90. Quoted in Jones, "Cybersleuths," p. 102.

91. Peter Olsen, telephone interview by the author, January 3, 2007.

92. Quoted in Jones, "Cybersleuths," p. 102.

93. Quoted in Deborah Radcliff, "Crime in the 21st Century," *InfoWorld*, December 14, 1998, p. 65.

94. Khan, December 15, 2006.

95. Quoted in Lisa Napoli, "The Kinko's Caper: Burglary by Modem," *New York Times*, August 7, 2003, p. 1G.

96. Lon, interview by the author, Burnsville, MN, November 28, 2006.

97. Lon, November 28, 2006.

98. Norah, January 18, 2007.

99. Nasset, December 12, 2006.

100. Quoted in Joe Light, "Agents Target Online Criminal Underground," *Boston Globe*, September 25, 2005, p. 6E.

101. Quoted in Light, "Agents Target Online Criminal Underground," p. 6E.

102. Roy, telephone interview, April 16, 2007.

103. Quoted in "Employees Are a Risk Factor for Identity Theft," *OfficePro*, Fall 2006, p. 2.

For More Information

Books

Frank W. Abagnale, *Catch Me if You Can: The Amazing True Story of the Youngest and Most Daring Con Man in the History of Fun and Profit*. New York: Broadway, 2000. The memoir of a notorious identity thief who successfully eluded international law enforcement agents for five years in the 1960s and eventually turned legitimate fraud detection consultant for the FBI. Abagnale's story is the basis for the 2002 feature film *Catch Me if You Can*.

J.A. Hitchcock, *Net Crimes and Misdemeanors: Outmaneuvering Web Spammers, Stalkers, and Con Artists*. Medford, NJ: Information Today/CyberAge, 2006. Excellent section on Internet scams, with a good index.

Rachel Lininger and Russell Dean Vines, *Phishing: Cutting the Identity Theft Line*. Indianapolis: Wiley, 2005. Challenging reading, but very complete information about the crime. For those who have a good background in computer technology.

Periodicals

Brooke A. Masters and Caroline Mayer, "Protect Your ID—and Pray," *Seattle Times*, December 8, 2002.

Tony Pugh, "Crooks Seem to Have Upper Hand in Identity Theft Crimes, Experts Say," *Knight Ridder/Tribune News Service*, June 29, 2005.

Paul F. Roberts, "Hackers Beware: You Are What You Type," *InfoWorld*, August 14, 2006.

Internet Sources

Jennifer Pero, "Who Are You?" *Government Security*, July 1, 2002. http://govtsecurity.com/mag.article_2/.

Oriana Zill, "Crossing Borders: How Terrorists Use Fake Passports," *PBS Frontline*. www.pbs.org/wgbh/pages/frontline/shows/trail/etc/fake.html.

Web Sites

Federal Trade Commission (www.consumer.gov/idtheft/). Offers advice to victims of identity theft as well as information for protecting against and fighting the crime. Also includes an online quiz to test whether you are being careful enough with personal information.

OnGuard Online (www.onguardonline.gov/phishing.html). This site provides a lot of information about phishing practices and detection. Discusses spyware and other online risks, too.

U.S Immigration and Customs Enforcement (www.ice.gov/pi/news/). Explains the various types of documents ICE agents process and the challenges of keeping those documents secure. Also gives useful insight into identity theft in connection with illegal immigration.

Index

Picture Credits

Cover image (main): © iStockphoto.com/Jose Luis Gutierrez

AP Images, 7, 13, 22, 31, 41, 46, 56, 64, 65, 75, 77

© Bettmann/CORBIS, 61

© Sam Diephuis/zefa/CORBIS, 35

© Muriel Dovic/CORBIS, 26

© Kim Kulish/CORBIS, 79, 82

© Reuters/CORBIS, 78

© Jeffrey L. Rotman/CORBIS, 68

© Chuck Savage/CORBIS, 18

Getty Images, 38

AFP/Getty Images, 44, 73

Philip J. Brittan/Getty Images, 49

Ghislain & Marie David de Lossey/Getty Images, 58

Richard Elliot/Getty Images, 21

Ross M. Horowitz/Getty Images, 15

Wathiq Khuzaie/Getty Images, 66

Frederic Lucano/Getty Images, 87

David McGlynn/Getty Images, 89

Ken Reid/Getty Images, 52

Uma Sanghvi/Getty Images, 50

Richard Shock/Getty Images, 33

Fredrik Skold/Getty Images, 84

Stockbyte/Getty Images, 53

Christian Thomas/Getty Images, 71

Steve Zmina, 10, 25, 39

About the Author

Gail B. Stewart received her undergraduate degree from Gustavus Adolphus College in St. Peter, Minnesota. She did her graduate work in English, linguistics, and curriculum study at the College of St. Thomas and the University of Minnesota. She taught English and reading for more than ten years.

She is the author of more than two hundred books for children and young adults. Stewart and her husband live in Minneapolis. They have three grown sons.